FRIDAY NIGHT HEROES

A Look At Texas High School Football

Carlton Stowers

EAKIN PRESS
Austin, Texas

Published in the United States of America
By Eakin Press, P.O. Box 23066, Austin, Texas 78735

ISBN 0-89015-401-5

To Larry,

*my brother, who happens also to be
my favorite high school football coach.*

ACKNOWLEDGMENTS

The author wishes to thank the publications in which these pieces originally appeared under his byline, though sometimes in slightly different form. The chapter on Brownwood High originally appeared in *Sports Illustrated*, the one on Asherton in *Parade*, and the Ken Hall profile was published by *Southwest Airlines Magazine*. The story on Kountze High first appeared in *People* and the pieces on Abilene High and Pflugerville were published by *Dave Campbell's Texas Football* while *Scene Magazine*, The Sunday supplement of the *Dallas Morning News*, published the pieces on Star High, Big Sandy, Johnny Jones' return to Lampasas, the Texas School for the Deaf, and the Texas-Mexico high school series. That each saw fit to print the stories in the first place is greatly appreciated.

TABLE OF CONTENTS

INTRODUCTION

Having now toiled at this business of sitting in front of a typewriter for a length of time proper to give me some small degree of tenure, I have come upon a number of major truths worthy of mentioning as I prepare to explain the reason for the book now in your hands.

While literary prizes that wait out there somewhere would be nice decoration for the wall and welcome salve for the ego, I am forced to admit that the primary reason for my writing is the gnawing urge to pound out the same style of life for my loved ones as the neighborhood breadwinners who mend damaged fenders, unravel the mysteries of computers and hawk insurance provide for theirs.

Those of us who have chosen the crapshoot business of freelance journalism are duty bound to peddle our wares wherever the marketplace is most active. Therefore, if *Pantyhose Review* is in dire need of fifteen hundred words and admits willingness to pay reasonably well, yes sir, the story's coming up. If certain editors, unmindful of your plans for a masterwork, call to suggest their readers simply can't do without a story on the magic and mystery of the feedlot industry, you simply hustle off to the closet, pick a pair of shoes you care little for, and hit the road.

Which is to say the guy — a writer of the kind of fiction that sells like hula hoops and silly putty once did, no doubt — who spread the rumor that this business of writing is glamorous should deservedly have unpardonable sins committed against him. And to those sometimes writers who regularly beg off assignments for lack of proper creative urges, we five-day-a-week hacks say bull and double-bull. This ain't no picnic, pal, even if it is a sit-down job for the most part.

And frustration isn't exactly a stranger. Deadlines, you should know, aren't the best live-in companions to have around. And it's no real fun to have your big plans for a work of substance and meaning interrupted by the urgency to dash off and interview some Hollywood starlet whose I.Q. and bust measurement are one and the same.

Which is as frank an admission as I know how to make of the fact there are several tons of magazine articles and books floating around out there that are hardly children their literary fathers are crazy about.

But enough of the dark side.

There are times when no pursuit in the Free World is as satisfying. What has been collected herein are some of the good times, the end results of satisfying experiences. And if you'll allow a moment of breast-beating, the pieces to follow are among those I personally judge the cream of a crop whose volume is beginning to cause me wonder. I have been labeled prolific by my peers and have yet to decide whether that is compliment or complaint. I simply view it as a necessary state of affairs. If attending more than one book at a time while constantly nudging magazine editors to learn their plans for next month's issue is a crime, I'm guilty. If the fall book list includes more than one title carrying my byline and a half dozen or so magazines reach the racks at the same time with pieces I've done, so be it and hip-hip-hooray. It pays the piper.

For out of it all, lo and behold, sometimes comes a sample of the kind of writing you wouldn't mind sending home to mother. I make no apologies for claiming what you're about to read fits that particular category.

The pieces in this tome are related only by a central theme: Texas high school football. It is an obsession of mine just as it is thousands upon thousands of other native Texans who take their Friday nights as seriously as the prime interest and oil depletion allowance. Sometimes more so. Provide me with the slightest excuse to put aside the worries of faulty plumbing, a throbbing headache, pressing literary matters or any other of man's daily miseries, and I'm game. Suggestion that the evening might be well spent in attendance at some high school stadium, there to watch teen-age boys act as certified community heroes for a couple of hours, and it'll only take me a minute to get my coat.

Thus, when it has been my happy chore to mix business with pleasure writing on the subject, I've come as close to the journalist's Camelot as the profession will allow.

These pieces, describing winners and losers, powerhouse teams with high paid coaches and the downtrodden whose only headlines are those signaling yet another futile effort, have been written over a span of several seasons. In the subsequent passage of time some of the winners have fallen on hard times. On the other hand, good fortune has finally taken it upon itself to shine on those whose bygone struggles are here described.

There was, at first, an urge to tinker with the structure of the stories, to bring them into present tense. But in an attempt to do so I found that the real timeliness was deluded, the spirit of the moment in which they were written lost. Thus better judgment prevailed and they are here pretty much in their original state, woven together as best I can weave pieces done at different times and different locations.

In the pages ahead you will, hopefully, learn something not only about sport at its most basic level but also become handshake familiar with a special breed of people.

I leave you to judge the literary merits. All I know is that it has been fun. And I challenge any Big Bucks bank president or high ranking member of the bomb-squad to try and convince me his is a better way to make a living.

— *Carlton Stowers*

1

"Hopefully, the future of our nation will fall into the hands of young men like these coached by Brownwood's Gordon Wood ... "

— *Lyndon B. Johnson*

A PRIDE OF LIONS

It's the last stop before you plunge headlong into cattle country, a Sinclair Lewis type community with street after street of modest white frame houses shaded by ancient pecan and walnut trees.

Brownwood, with its tall church spires and Rebekah Lodge rummage sales and monthly rasslin' matches and a small college campus which has known neither violence nor nationwide notoriety, is but sixteen miles removed from the geographic center of Texas.

There is a recently completed school for wayward girls, a Holiday Inn, a new shopping center, and for those in search of nightlife, the Pizza Hut, Mercury Bowling Lanes, Bresler's 33 Flavors Ice Cream Parlor or one of the 7-11 Stores where you can pick up a six pack. Or the drive-in movie which the city's self-appointed morality guardians once took legal action against to prevent the showing of Academy Award winner, "Midnight Cowboy."

Which is to say it is not greatly unlike most other Texas towns whose population is listed in the neighborhood of 17,000. God, country, motherhood and Bible Belt conservatism are still very much alive and well in Brownwood, just as surely as the channel and bluecat

1

bite early in the mornings down on the Pecan Bayou.

Though it attracts an occasional FHA convention or a gathering of regional wildlife conservationists or competitors for the tournaments regularly held by the local bass club, it must be noted that Brownwood hardly ranks alongside the Astrodome or Neiman-Marcus as one of the stops a vacationer might plan to make while visiting Texas. It's still a good two hours on to Johnson City, hometown of the late politician of note, and the fast-pace life of Dallas is 200 miles north on Interstate 67.

The city has, however, made its contribution to the legacy of the Lone Star State. In a tradition long upheld by relatively small Texas towns, Brownwood's high school football players have personally seen to it that their community is more than a tiny dot on one of Humble's giveaway maps.

In a state where school boy football is oft-times a six-point favorite over Sunday-go-to-meetin', Brownwood is the current Mother Church. The Brownwood High School Lions, five-time state champions, are the primary preoccupation of every citizen physically able to jam himself into the 8,000-seat Cen-Tex Stadium on autumn Friday nights or book passage on the chartered bus which Coggin Avenue Baptist pastor Leon Aduddell drives to such destinations as Temple or Burkburnett or Weatherford. Curfew at the Golden Age Rest Home is disregarded when Ken Schulze, radio station KBWD's Voice of the Lions, is doing the play-by-play.

Downtown merchants decorate their windows in maroon and white and display their latest stock alongside a glossy photo or two of the town's teenage heroes and if one sees a car which doesn't bear a bumper sticker telling that its driver is a Lion Booster it must be assumed that it is from out of town.

Even for a state which still spends untold man-hours a year arguing whether Doak Walker or Warren McVea was the best broken field runner in schoolboy history, Brownwood is unique. To say that its high school is just

2

another of the 1,000 public schools in Texas playing 500 games each fall before an estimated annual attendance of 10,000,000 would not be greatly unlike referring to the Siege of the Alamo as just another one of history's wartime battles.

In talking with the townspeople one must assume that if truly there exist wards of Heaven, the maroon and white Brownwood Lions qualify hands down.

But it has not always been so.

Tradition has demanded that teams should rise from the Texas schoolboy ranks to become dominant powers. They've been known at various stages of history as The Greatest Team Ever, The Team Nobody Can Beat, etc., and have gone to battle draped in every color of the rainbow. In the '20s, Waco ruled, winning 73 of 78 games in a six-year period and defeated Latin Cathedral of Cleveland, Ohio, for the mythical national prep championship of 1927.

By 1937 tiny Hull-Daisetta, one of the numerous rural consolidated schools, had gone 43 games without a single defeat. Then came the Amarillos and the Wichita Falls and the Baytowns. Oil rich Breckenridge had its day in the early '50s, winning four state championships in six years. Abilene High stepped into the spotlight in the mid-'50s and established a national winning streak record of 49 in a row, an achievement which earned its coach, Chuck Mosher, a $9,000 bonus from an obviously pleased booster club and a writeup in *Time* magazine. Four years later the same publication was dispatching a writer to little Pflugerville, a school with an enrollment of 88, which had stretched the national record to 55 straight.

The record has since passed on to such football hotbeds as Massillon, Ohio, and Jefferson City, Missouri, but those who worship at the shrine of Texas high school football will quickly point out to you that the only reason such long term winning streaks have gone out of style is that virtually *all* teams in Texas are of high quality, thus eliminating the possibility of a "patsy" schedule for anyone.

High school football doesn't merely arrive in Texas each September. Rather, it explodes, from the barren cold of the Panhandle to the piney woods of East Texas to the muggy heat of the Gulf Coast. It is not a phenomenon to be taken lightly. To wit:

Several years ago Hurricane Beulah hit the South Texas community of Three Rivers, flooding the high school football field and ruining all the team's equipment. Three Rivers school officials pled with their counterparts at archrival George West High to postpone their upcoming game but George West, seeing the possibility of a district championship, demanded a forfeit. It marked Three Rivers' first defeat of the season, officially recorded as a 0-1 loss.

It hasn't been too many years since Magnolia High School was penalized because its elementary school coach was caught in the act of conducting spring practice and Corsicana High found itself in trouble when it became public knowledge that over-exuberant citizens were supplying the players with vitamin pills and footing *all* medical bills for their young warriors. Then there was the rival team which reported that it had evidence that Robert Lewis, the leading rusher for the Conroe Tigers, had, in fact, reached his eighteenth birthday before the September first deadline and thus should be declared ineligible. An investigation followed and the truth finally surfaced. Lewis was most certainly too old — by a grand total of eight hours — and he went to the study hall for the remainder of the season.

They still talk about the father of a standout halfback who repeatedly insisted to a Breckenridge oil company that he did not want to move to the West Texas community so that his son could score a few touchdowns for the Battlin' Buckaroos. Returning from a weekend trip, however, he found that his farmhouse had been lifted from its foundation and moved fifty miles down the road to Breckenridge. If he wished to move it back,

4

he was told, it was okay, but would be done at his own expense. Thus his son became a member in good standing of one of the legendary Buckaroo teams.

Some indication of the devotion with which Texans pursue the weekly schoolboy mini-wars is mirrored in the fact that both the Associated Press and United Press International release weekly high school Top Tens which are read with as much interest as those which rank the top college teams from week to week.

The Texas Interscholastic League, governing body of high school athletics, goes the NCAA one better, however, and provides a playoff schedule designed to determine the true No. 1 teams in Classes AAAA, AAA, AA, A, B and in six-and eight-man ball.

A silver-plated football mounted on a walnut base is the Texas schoolboy's answer to the Grantland Rice Trophy, MacArthur Bowl, etc., and is earned only after 48 minutes of supreme effort on some neutral field in what is referred to as the State Finals — the fifteenth game of the year for the two teams which manage to earn the right to play for the championship.

For a span of forty years Brownwood High School could not even so much as handle district rivals like Graham and Stephenville and Vernon, much less level any kind of offensive attack on the remainder of the schoolboy football world. Even in the '20s when coach Mack Miller went over to boom towns like Cisco and Ranger and brought back players to live in rooms rented from sports-minded residents, fortunes rarely reached the .500 mark. That the heroics of an elusive running back named Chili Rice made him something of a living legend in the '40s apparently made little difference to opponents who regularly found a way of defeating the luckless Lions.

"The Lions," recalls Groner Pitts, the world's funniest mortician and one of the resident experts on past Brownwood glories, "spent most of their lives facing third and long."

5

Thus it was that the city's gridiron history prior to 1960 is referred to as Before Gordon Wood. And if that seems to bear certain religious innuendos, well, so be it. Until he was hired only one district championship trophy had been won by the school in four decades.

The search for a man with a reputation of building a winner began and ended with Wood, a hound dog jowled man with sunken eyes which are at times Sonny Liston sullen, then five minutes later will turn soft and smiling.

His references dated back to 1938 when he had begun his coaching career in the dry-bed West Texas town of Spur and wound through other rural whistle-stops where he directed the fortunes of the Rule Bobcats, the Roscoe Plowboys, Seminole Indians, Winters Blizzards and then Stamford where during his seven-year stay he saw his Bulldogs win two Class AA championships and post 35 consecutive wins during one productive period. When the Brownwood school board caught up with him he had just finished his second successful season at Victoria.

Gordon Wood's suits never quite look freshly pressed and to the casual acquaintance he hardly comes on as the dynamic leader who can convince 17-year-old boys they are just a notch below Superman, yet a lifetime coaching record of 383 wins, 77 losses and 11 ties stands as material testimony to his ability.

Today district championships are but a stepping-stone to the November and December playoffs.

In the carefully chronicled annals of Texas schoolboy football history, dating back to 1900 when two non-school sponsored Dallas teams played without the blessings of their respective superintendents, thus setting in motion all this madness, no coach had won more than four state titles before Gordon Wood.

He has won nine.

Owner Bob Dunn sat in one of the back booths at his Palace Drug, re-hashing the holiday bowl outcomes and remarking on the respective coaching genius of men like Paul "Bear" Bryant, Woody Hayes and Darrell Royal.

Rodger Sweeney, a car salesman, golfing friend of Wood, and public address announcer for the Lions games, listened intently, then joined the conversation, pointing out that he personally would like to see the whole lot of them bring some of their $35,000-$40,000 genius down here in the high school ranks where you have to make do with a 147-pound fullback with something less than blazing speed and see how many championships they could stack up.

His implication was clear.

"Darrell," he says, "was here to speak at our football banquet a few years ago and he said that in his estimation the best coaching being done in the country is by high school coaches. Particularly those in Texas."

At age 59, chances are that Gordon Wood isn't likely to ever see the day when he occupies the head coaching chair at some major college. World War II, he feels, cheated him out of that.

A defensive end of modest achievement back when Hardin-Simmons still listed football as one of the activities for its students, Wood was summoned to Spur High School following graduation where he spent two years as an assistant to coach Blackie Wadzek, earning the princely sum of $73.25 per month. When Wadzek retired Wood applied for the head job but was turned down. In retrospect, it is worth noting that the school board members who decided Wood was not yet ready to assume the responsibilities of a head coach came to their decision on April Fool's Day.

While Spur was hiring a man named W. W. Duckworth, Gordon Wood was landing his first head job, 75 miles down the highway at Rule.

"The first thing I did when I got the job," Wood remembers, "was to schedule a game with Spur. Then, after I persuaded Coach Duckworth to play us I immediately began to wonder if I hadn't been a little carried away with the idea of showing that school board they had made a mistake."

7

Rule High School boasted no tradition of winning and was hardly a fountain of youthful talent. No sooner had the season begun than Wood lost four players to grades, one moved away, and he was faced with playing a youngster at tackle who had never even seen a football game.

"On the other hand, we did have four kids who were pretty big and had some ability," he says, "so I felt we had a chance.

"We went over to Spur and were asked if we would like to attend their pep rally. I said we would like to come but before going out to the school I stopped off at the hotel and put our four big kids up in a room and told them not to leave. Then I took the sixteen little kids we had to the pep rally."

Duckworth, taken aback by the lack of size of Wood's squad, launched into a pep talk directed toward the team he was to play against later in the evening. "You fellas are small but I'm sure you'll give it everything you've got. We'll do everything in our power to make sure no one gets hurt tonight."

Wood expressed his gratitude for the consideration of his rival coach, went by the hotel to pick up the remainder of his squad, and began final preparations for the game.

History shows that on that particular evening Spur managed only two first downs as Wood's rag-knot Rule team won, 27-0.

A couple of seasons later the Japanese, obviously not the least concerned with the outcome of the District 8-B football race, bombed Pearl Harbor. Suddenly the engagements Wood's Bobcats were fighting were placed in a new perspective. The townspeople were suddenly more concerned with youngsters who were trading their shoulder pads and letter jackets for battle gear of another style.

By 1945 many former Bobcats were marching back to Rule but Chief Petty Officer Gordon Wood, faced with

8

the realization that if he hoped to continue coaching it meant starting all over again in some other dusty little West Texas town, loaded his dufflebag aboard a bus and headed for Roscoe.

"I'll always believe the real years for my advancement," he says in a matter-of-fact tone which now hints neither of remorse nor bitterness, "would have been the time I spent in the service. Tugboat Jones (a revered if not poetic name in Texas schoolboy coaching annals) took over my job there at Rule and when I got back he was coaching at Wichita Falls High, one of the biggest schools in the state."

Thus the stages upon which Wood was to show his early day coaching ability were the grassbur-infested stadium in Seminole and the roping arena-turned-football field in Winters until Stamford, a community of less than 5,000 where kids learn the Bulldog Fight Song before they get around to the Pledge of Allegiance, beckoned.

Winning was everything in Stamford, Texas, long before Vince Lombardi ever bought a home in Green Bay. The youngsters of the community spend their elementary days dreaming of the time they will wear the blue and white and do their part for the glory of the Bulldogs.

Wood hit town selling the resident youngsters on the idea that the prime ingredient for winning was confidence. They bought his philosophy by the truckload.

Early in one particularly rough playoff game, Charlie Davis, the team's top runner, walked into the opposing team's huddle and in all sincerity informed them that "y'all might as well play clean, 'cause we're gonna beat you anyway."

There is no recollection of the sportsmanship or lack of same exhibited by the opponents that day but it is duly noted that the Bulldogs won handily.

A few years later an injury-riddled Stamford team traveled to Brownwood and found itself trailing late in the final period and backed up on its own one-yard line. Wood sent center Wendell Robinson into the game with

9

instructions to tell the quarterback to run three plunges into the line, then punt them out of trouble.

Robinson trotted into the huddle and calmly told the quarterback that "Coach Wood said for you to jes' follow me 99 yards for a touchdown." So the youngster proceeded to run the length of the field on the next play, scoring a touchdown that was to lift the team to victory.

By 1957 Wood had captured two Class AA championships, handed the reins to assistant Larry Wartes, and headed for the Gulf Coast in search of a new challenge.

In Victoria, Gordon Wood was out of place. The state of Texas is subdivided into regions with their own particular customs and mores and Wood was every bit a West Texan, a product of a breezy, set-jawed, independent, a-man-works-for-his-dollar heritage. In Victoria football was something less than a life-and-death matter.

"All my life," Wood explains, "I had been dealing with farmers and ranchers. Hell, I could go sit out in a pickup or lean up against the barn and talk to everyone in town, from the mayor to the school janitor.

"In Victoria I was suddenly dealing with the Country Club set and it bothered me. I remember one time when one of the girls in school invited my daughter, Pat, to dinner and a movie. I didn't think much about it until she came home and told me that the dinner had been for eighteen girls and was at the Country Club.

"My wife and I sat down and told her there was just no way we could ever entertain like that. Hell, money's always been one of the least important things to me all my life and suddenly I was thinking about how to keep up with the Joneses.

"And, too, there was the attitude toward the football program. We were playing a San Antonio school in a game that was to decide the district championship and sold only 250 adult tickets. I began to wonder what it would be like if we had a bad season and decided I wasn't going to wait around to find out."

The Brownwood school board offered him the oppor-

10

tunity to return to more familiar surroundings where a man could concentrate his entire efforts on coaching football.

Now there is a feeling that Gordon Wood could, if he so chose, run for mayor and win by two touchdowns.

Prior to 1972 the home field for Wood's young warriors was Lions Stadium, a rickety steel and wood structure which Urban Renewal passed by. During any fall week it would be the site of a couple of junior high games, a B-team game, a junior varsity game, a varsity game and was finally set to rest for the week after Howard Payne College had performed on Saturday. More than one visiting coach remarked on the fact that the turf was more suited for roller derby than football.

Local supporters would regularly write irate letters to the editor about the condition of the stadium and the lack of parking facilities, then purchase 1,800 season tickets each year.

"For a helluva long time," says Stuart Coleman, the Coors beer distributor, "we had the best team and the worst stadium in four-A ball. It was embarrassing to invite out-of-town friends in to see the Lions play in a place like that."

There were even those who felt that if a better playing site was not soon forthcoming the city stood to lose Wood as a coach. After all, hadn't Class AAAA powerhouse San Angelo Central asked him down for an interview then held up on talking to any other candidates for a week while Wood pondered their offer?

Thus things shifted into high gear. A group of businessmen gathered around the table at the Chamber of Commerce office and began laying plans for a new 8,000-seat stadium. Rather than risk the possible failure of a bond election they decided it best to build the stadium primarily with donated funds.

Here's how it was done:

The Brownwood Independent School District, Howard Payne College, Brown County and the City of

11

Brownwood agreed to provide a total of $250,000 in funds and labor. The city came up with a site about a mile south of town in the old Camp Bowie area, once a hub of activity during World War II. The Brownwood school system and Howard Payne would lease the stadium from the stadium corporation for ten years, but to provide starting capital, the First National Bank agreed to loan them the amount of the lease, interest free.

Local fans were offered reserved seat options, the price being $100. Calvin Fryar, chairman of the stadium steering committee, points to the fact that that project alone produced $70,000.

The family of the late Wendell Mayes, former owner of KBWD and a died-in-the-wool Lions supporter, contributed $25,000 for a press box which would feature carpeting, central heat and air and elaborate viewing booths for press, radio and photographers.

When the bids were let, local contractor Herman Bennett, a long time season ticket holder, beat the nearest competitor by $90,000 and was the only one of the four bidders who guaranteed completion of the structure before the start of the 1972 season.

He then turned around and joined eight other businessmen who donated $10,000 to the project.

Numerous other individuals made lesser contributions and scores offered their time and special skills to help see the project become a reality.

Brick to build the concession stands, ticket booth and restrooms was given by the Texas Brick Company and light towers were gifts from Brownwood Television Cable and Andrews Tower Company. Tom Lafferty Electric did all the electrical work for cost and Jimmy and Sid Cole, local home builders, seeded the playing field.

Players, coaches, parents, fans, businessmen and school officials would gather in the summer evenings to paint, hoe weeds and tend to many of the numerous chores that needed to be done before the stadium could be made ready to play in.

It stands today as a monument to community spirit and unabashed devotion to the game the townspeople cherish.

Still, it should be noted that Brownwood lacks the financial quick-draw of many Texas communities and thus its teams still travel by chartered bus to out-of-town games while several teams from larger schools occasionally fly.

Wichita Falls Hirschi, a member of the same district in which Brownwood competes, plays all its home games in a 20,000-seat, synthetic-turfed public stadium.

Wood has seen his salary increase steadily since winning the 1960 state championship with a team which did not have a boy on the roster weighing as much as 180 pounds, yet he is still $3,000 shy of the $17,500 paid Andrews High head coach Jimmie Keeling in 1971. Nor does he have a free automobile at his disposal, having instead to use his '68 Buick whenever one of the school's driver's education cars isn't available.

This is not to say, however, that Brownwood High's athletic program should be compared to, say, that at Hempstead, Long Island, where the school spends $2,400 a year on its football program.

Indeed, that figure would barely pay for the hydrotherapy whirlpool machine ($450) and the ultrasonic muscle-healer ($950) which are part of the modern training room equipment at Brownwood High. Certainly it would not outfit the four high school squads (varsity, junior varsity, and two B-teams) where every youngster is issued about $250 worth of equipment.

Organized football begins in the seventh grade in Brownwood and most other Texas school systems with qualified coaches teaching the same basic theories Wood delivers to his elder Lions. By the time a youngster has reached the varsity he is quite ready to comprehend, digest and set to memory the 100 different plays and eight offensive sets which are to be found in Wood's mimeographed playbook.

"Football," says Wood, "is just more important here in Texas. It's a tradition; almost a heritage. A daddy played for Brownwood High so his son is playing now and in not too many years *his* son will be playing.

"Yes, we take it seriously."

Which is perhaps the chief reason behind the much publicized claim that the best schoolboy football to be found in the U.S. is bred and fed in Texas. In an attempt to substantiate that boast the state has in the past sent its all-star teams up against outside forces and returned home to heroes' welcomes.

Wichita Falls is the site of an annual summer all-star game called the Oil Bowl, matching the top graduating seniors from Texas and Oklahoma. Texas holds a woefully lopsided edge in the series which dates back to 1945. In the early '60s, Pennsylvania, another state which claims superior quality high school football (along with Ohio, California and Louisiana), extended a challenge for Texas to pick its best 33 graduating seniors and meet in a game in Hershey, Pennsylvania. After Texas, coached by NFL Hall of Fame quarterback Bobby Layne, scored consecutive wins of 26-10, 34-2 and 45-14, the series died from lack of interest on the part of the Pennsylvania ticket buyers.

It was almost a decade ago that Bill Smith, a Houston construction magnate, provided $18,000 for Huntsville High to travel to Anchorage, Alaska, and engage the top Alaskan prep team. Huntsville, which had lost regularly during its season back home, scored a two touchdown victory. No Texas team was ever invited back and the "annual" Santa Claus Bowl never rode again.

Wood will tell you that there are numerous reasons for the high caliber of Texas schoolboy football. "We've got better weather here than in most states," he begins, "and there is more interest on the part of the community. Our equipment is a little more sophisticated than most. And, then, we have the playoff system and the all-star game to provide the kids with goals to shoot at.

"Also, there are more outstanding coaches in high school ball here in Texas. This is one of the few states where a man can remain on the high school level and still make a living. In most states it is just a stepping stone. If you don't get into college coaching or administration work after a few years, you starve or sell insurance."

Some indication of the satisfaction he feels in his job is mirrored in the fact that despite spending two months each summer coaching the linebackers for the Winnipeg Blue Bombers of the Canadian Professional League, he has repeatedly turned down offers to make it a full time position. Instead, he returns home in late July to begin preparations for another schoolboy season.

Jim Spavital, head coach of the Bombers, met Wood when both were stationed in California during the war. "Gordon was in charge of recruiting players for the Naval team and I had played freshman ball at Oklahoma A&M before enlisting," he says. "He would sit around talking football to anyone who would listen. His knowledge of the game even at that stage was staggering.

"When I got this job I tried to hire him. He's the kind of man a professional football coaching staff needs. When we get the kids together for pre-season practice, it's necessary to weed out the non-players as quickly as possible. You have to be hard and demanding — and occasionally you will lose a really good player simply because you've been such a son-of-a-bitch that he just doesn't feel like taking it any longer.

"I'd venture to say that Gordon has saved six or eight players for me in the past few years. He'll seek out the boy with his head down and about ready to pack up and go home and have a talk with him. God, he's magnificent at that. He'll go up to one of those big ol' kids and put his arm around him and start talking in that soft Southern drawl of his and, hell, the next day the kid's back on the playing field playing like King Kong.

"That's Gordon's main gift, communication. He is sincere, honest and the type person the players believe in. He's the stabilizing factor in a situation where almost everyone a kids turn to seems 100 per cent against him."

If the name Gordon Lenear Wood is not familiar in the nation's sport-crazed households, it is at least well-known in football circles. A coach in Anaheim, California, spends his summers running and re-running films of Brownwood High games mailed him by Wood. Several other coaches in California, Pennsylvania, Oklahoma and New Mexico correspond with him regularly, asking endless questions about his approach to his chosen craft. School superintendents in search of a new head coach begin their search by calling Wood and asking first if he is interested and then, after receiving a negative response, asking for him to make recommendations. A coach in Lubbock, troubled by marital problems, called on Wood for advice.

At coaching clinics he is as popular as the nearest nightspot. During a post-season clinic recently, Wood shared the podium with several of the nation's outstanding college coaches and his lecture was attended by a standing-room-only crowd. A well-known receiver coach who had been a legend in his professional days was scheduled to follow Wood and found himself speaking to an almost empty room as most of the coaches followed Wood into the lobby to ask additional questions.

"I was at a coaching clinic last summer," says Ted Plumb, a former Texas high school coach now on the staff at the University of Kansas, "and saw Gordon mingling with people like John McKay and Woody Hayes and Darrell Royal and the thought suddenly crossed my mind that Wood, in his own quiet way just might be the best coach in the bunch. And I don't think you would find that I'm the only person in the world who things that way, either."

When Wood talks about his profession he is a man constantly in search of converts. Anyone who approaches the game at less than full throttle is of little use to him.

He recalled a clinic not too many years ago when an Eastern high school coach delivered such observations as "a pass is nothing but a long fumble" and "the kicking game is silly; soccer is a kicking game." Wood cannot tell you what the remainder of the coach's talk contained. He walked out. "That guy isn't a football coach," he says, "he's a damn clown.

"I had one high school coach from Canada tell me about a game his kids won and then he went on to describe how proud he was that they also won the beer-drinking contest afterwards. Hell, he'd get fired on the spot if he tried something like that in Texas.

"I know a coach in Ohio who owns three beer joints. That would never do in our system. We're a little more strait-laced."

In a time when the leadership of the nation's high schools is turning to the hands of the long-haired rock group performers and there is a liberal trend which insists that a coach be prepared to bend with the change or be broken by it, there has been little revision in Wood's coaching philosophy. Maybe his kids no longer wear flat-tops, appreciate dress codes or carry Chip Hilton hard-backs under their arms but, whether they admit it or not, by today's standards they are old-fashioned seven-teen-and eighteen-year-olds.

While the students of Dallas's Woodrow Wilson High were trying to convince their school officials that they felt there were too many pep rallies and that things like spirit ribbons have no meaning for them any longer, it remains a constant chore at Brownwood High to keep enthusiasm for football from boiling to such a point that academic pursuit becomes secondary.

"You have to envy the role of the coach and his athletes in the small schools today," says Woodrow Wilson principal Wayne Pierce. "When I was coaching in the early '60s the athlete played because he was somebody, a

17

leader in the school. Now only in the smaller schools does an athlete stick out like that."

Which could well be a primary reason that Wood has repeatedly turned down offers to assume the coaching duties at larger metropolitan schools.

"Sure we've had some changes at Brownwood," Wood will admit. "I see some big ol' boy walking down the hall and have to ask myself why he's not doing anything but attending class and hanging around on the JRB Food Store parking lot in the afternoons while some 140-pounder is out there with us, sweating and hurting. And we have some girls who are called into the office and told to go home and put on a bra or a longer skirt. There are some kids going to school who don't care anything about our football team; they resent it, in fact, because it gets so much attention.

"That big kid I was telling you about goes downtown and a half dozen people will ask him why he's not playing football and pretty soon he's pretty hostile about the whole thing. You just have to accept that and concentrate on doing the best you can for those who are interested.

"We're just about as demanding on our players as we always have been. There is something to the feeling that in a big school athletics are in competition with a lot of other things. We have outside activities that pull attention away from our program, too, but we rely a lot on self-discipline rather than imposing it to keep boys in the program.

"Of course," he concludes, "we also have the advantage of a tradition here. It's a lot easier to keep them interested and motivated when you're winning."

For now, Brownwood High's Lions rank as the prime example of Texas schoolboy excellence.

Yet while Lion ex's such as Lawrence Elkins (former Baylor All-America and No. 1 draft pick of the Houston Oilers) and Robert Young (former Oiler and Denver Broncos line standout) have achieved fame beyond their high school days, Brownwood is hardly the football factory college coaches dream about.

The most recent championship team, for instance, featured a 5-4, 143-pound tailback and a 5-6, 147-pound fullback, hardly measurements that will make the University of Texas fans forget Steve Worster.

Though there are about 990 students in the high school, tryouts for the football team have reached such a number that those who obviously don't have the ability to play are urged to pursue other avenues. "We try to give them all a fair chance," Wood says, "but when it is obvious that a boy is wasting his and our time, I have one of my assistants tell him maybe it would be best for him to give it up. It's a lousy thing for me to put off on one of the other coaches but I just don't have the heart to do it."

If a youngster insists, however, that he wants to be a part of the team even in face of the fact he isn't likely to see any playing action he is allowed to remain on the squad or serve as a manager.

Players are repeatedly reminded by Wood of the value of such virtues as dedication, determination and positive thinking. "We like our kids to get the idea they can play with anybody," Wood says. "I don't want them awed by anyone."

After his larger Temple High team had lost an early season game to Brownwood a couple of years ago, coach John Elam spent the remainder of the year showing the film of the game to his players. "Brownwood," he says, "plays the game the way it is supposed to be played. Their performance against us was better than any teaching film you can find on the market."

Wood does not come on as the complex individual local legend-makers would have you believe. Each Friday prior to a game he takes a 30-minute nap before slipping into the same brown "good luck" suit and eats the same pre-game meal of bacon and scrambled eggs, but that is the extent of his superstitions.

19

Many of his coaching tactics are straight out of the Knute Rockne days. During half time of a game which was promising to turn into disaster for his Lions several years ago he gathered his players around, waited for silence, pulled a letter from his coat pocket and began to read: "Dear Coach Wood: I am ninety-three years old and live in a rest home so I don't get to go to the Lions games anymore. But I listen to them on the radio and I love every one of those boys. The Lions make me proud and give me something to live for. God bless you and the Fighting Brownwood Lions . . ."

End of half time speech; beginning of a comeback that was to leave yet another Lions opponent smothered in defeat.

Bob Dunn insists that Wood has cost him and his Palace Drug a fortune in napkins alone. When holding court in the back booth, Wood must be able to diagram the particular play or formation he is discussing. He'll go to great lengths to explain the principle of the power sweep to anyone who shows the slightest interest.

If there is magic in Wood's approach it must be in his understanding of the boys he works with. "I think," he insists, "high school boys can sometimes be better than they think they possibly can."

During 30 years of working with youngsters he has learned to attack virtually any problem from its most vulnerable angle. If the situation calls for it, he is taut, controlled, driving.

"Last year we had a damn good player sit on the bench for two games," recalls Rodger Sweeny, "because he lost his head against Abilene Cooper, took a swing at a kid, and drew a penalty for unsportsman-like conduct. Gordon didn't just pull him out of the game. He sent him to the dressing room."

On the other hand he can be loose, free-wheeling and unpredictable.

"I called Gordon before our playoff game with him," remembers Lubbock Estacado High coach Pete Murray, a former Wood aide during the '60s, "and told him we wanted to use a Wilson ball when we were on offense. I knew they used another brand and just wanted to be sure they had one of our kind when we got there.

"So he comes out just a minute or two before the kickoff and says, 'Pete, this is the only Wilson we had; and pitches me this beat-up old thing with the cover peeling and the seams bustin' out all to hell.

"He got a big kick out of it, then told me he had already given a new Wilson to the referee. Imagine. Here I am in the playoffs for the first time, nervous as all get-out, and he's playing jokes and laughing up a storm because he's been there so many times before he knows damn well he's gonna swamp you before the afternoon's over."

Lions workouts are conducted like military maneuvers with no wasted time and all phases of preparation receiving daily attention. A youngster is given five minutes from the time the bell frees him from the classroom to be in his uniform lest he find himself running post-workout laps around the practice field.

If you are dismissed from the team you don't return. Well, almost never.

Perry Young, the youngest brother of pro player Robert and former Texas Tech standout Doug, found adhering to all the rules and regulations of competitive athletics too demanding and after several warnings was dismissed from the squad.

Brother Doug, upon hearing of Perry's fate, put in a long distance call to Wood and proceeded to plead his brother's case. He mentioned such facts as their parents' divorce which Perry was having a hard time adjusting to.

Wood countered by detailing particular incidents where Perry had been cautioned and, in fact, had been given the benefit of the doubt. Having heard Wood's side of the story Doug admitted that the coach had been more than fair, then added, "I just know this, Coach: If

21

you don't help him, no one will. I'd like for you to think about it."

The following day in the privacy of Wood's office Perry agreed to run forty laps a day for forty days to regain a spot on the team. As a footnote it should be mentioned that in his senior year he caught 21 passes for touchdowns and was selected to the All-State team.

"Over the long haul," says Wood, who admits he has perhaps mellowed some in his philosophy, "I suppose that is what high school football coaching is all about."

Though confident in my belief that the piece had been both accurate and a positive one, tenure in the writing profession convinced me that there would be those who felt, for reasons I would be unable to understand, that I had done my birthplace some grave injustice.

Still, I was anxious to observe the results of a national publication's invasion on the relative privacy of the community.

It was, then, with mixed emotions that I learned the story would arrive on the Palace Drug magazine rack the very Friday I had hoped to drive over and watch the Lions as they tried to solidify their District 4-AAA lead by defeating the Weatherford Kangaroos.

Every fifteen minutes during the day KBWD disc jockey Dallas Houston would interrupt somebody like the Nitty Gritty Dirt Band or Tom T. Hall to remind folks out there in radioland that the magazine was on sale and going fast. A reproduction of the first page of the article was splashed across the front page of the *Brownwood Bulletin.* By noon I had developed a monumental case of cold feet and was firmly convinced that Thomas Wolfe had hit the nail squarely on the head. I decided the best place for me that particular Friday night was hard by the fireplace and radio, safely removed from whatever reaction my literary efforts might have invoked. Chicken, I believe, was the term the lady of the house used.

Throughout the day I repeatedly resisted the urge to

place a call to a trusted friend in Brownwood and see if he had felt any tremors. By mid-afternoon I was seriously considering some other line of work when Trusted Friend called, saying he just thought I might like to know that everyone he had talked to really liked the story and, oh by the way, he had taken the liberty of telling radio announcer Ken Schulze that I would probably be tickled to death to be his halftime guest during the broadcast that evening.

Thus, flying squarely into the teeth of Wolfe and gripping self-doubt I made the trip to Brownwood.

Much to my relief I was greeted neither as a Conquering Hero nor a Bearded Judas. While watching the teams go through their respective pregame warmups an elderly gentleman sitting next to me struck up a conversation which eventually led to his asking if I had seen the story. "No," I lied bravely, "how was it?"

"Not bad," he said in a tone that not even your paranoid author could mistake for a rave, "but I sure wish't they'd used more pictures."

I never bothered to introduce myself.

Let it be said, however, that Volume 35, No. 18 of *Sports Illustrated* left its mark. To wit:

To illustrate the piece, S.I. photographer Lane Stewart, a good ol' boy from Fort Worth who went off to New York to seek fame and fortune, spent a week shooting no less than seventy rolls of film in Brownwood, winding up his photographic orgy at the Brownwood vs. Abilene game.

Wood's Lions fumbled a record seven times that evening and were defeated.

While it was the general contention that Abilene should indeed have received due credit for the win, I need not tell you who was handed credit for the loss in some of the more private Brown County conversations. My only consolation was in the fact that it had not been a district game.

After the article appeared, a columnist for the *San*

Angelo Standard Times dealt considerable wordage to the musical question, "Why can't those Eastern writers come to Texas and just write the facts rather than being so uppity and try to make us sound like a bunch of hicks?" (At that writing I had never been farther north than the Red River and that wayward journey was the result of a wrong turn just outside Henrietta.) An *Austin American* writer had a helluva opportunity to even the score when he called it "the best piece ever done on Texas high school football." Unfortunately, his observation was made to a fellow writer after one too many Coors and didn't make the morning edition. Or, for that matter, any edition.

Perry Young, the All-State receiver I had mentioned, visited a local lawyer to ask if he could sue since the article had mentioned the fact that his parents were divorced; my grandfather, a lifetime resident of Brownwood, mentioned that if he had known the kind of article I was going to write he could have given me "some really good stuff," and Bill Stovall, sports editor of the *Bulletin,* wrote at season's end that "while the article brought some long overdue recognition to the city, the team and Coach Wood, it did have some ill effects on the concentration of the players."

Still, the Lions managed to put together a 10-2 season and missed a possible sixth state championship when Plano kicked a field goal in the last 15 seconds to win the Class AAA semifinal game, 10-8.

A kind lady at *Sports Illustrated,* perhaps sensing that my id and ego were locked in mortal combat, salved some of my wounds by forwarding a bundle of letters which had arrived from satisfied customers in places like Pensacola, Omaha, Kansas City, Staten Island and Edmonton, Alberta. With the exception of a correspondent from Teaneck, New Jersey, who suggested that subjecting seventeen-year-old boys to such pressures (not to mention some writer having gall enough to glamorized it!) deserved rank right up there with Original Sin, the national opinion seemed to be that it was nice to know that there were still Brownwoods somewhere in this world.

Sometime later, after the season had ended, I was again in Brownwood on a Christmas shopping expedition. Somewhere between the rapid repeating crack-fire rifles and women's ready-to-wear, I bumped into Gordon Wood.

"Got time for a cup of coffee?" he asked. I nodded.

We sat for some time, re-hashing the season, discussing the financial giant step Charles Coody, a former quarterback for Wood at Stamford, had taken since winning the Masters golf championship, sharing holiday plans and generally keeping the conversation light and noncommital.

He asked if I had heard about the new emblems the Brownwood Jaycees had purchased for their blazers, noting they were in the shape of a football and had "Brownwood, Home of Texas's Best High School Football Team" embroidered on them. And did I know about the New Jersey group which had called to see if Brownwood was interested in a post-season challenge game with its favorite high school team?

From time to time he shuffled his feet as though anxious to get moving. I felt there was something else on his mind, however, so I held my ground and accepted the waitresses refill of my cup.

"You know," he finally said, measuring his words as carefully as if he were sending in a play from the sidelines, "during the season about the only thing I can think about is our football team. I let a lot of things go that should be attended to . . . "

"It's a full-time job," I acknowledged.

"Well, anyway, what I wanted to say was I should have gotten in touch with you about that story you wrote. It was really nice and I just wanted to let you know I appreciated it."

25

He said he would like to send me a couple of tickets to the Lions home opener in their new stadium next fall. I assured him I'd be there and left not only with great peace of mind but also the knowledge of where I'd be on the first Friday night of the next season.

" 'I'm surprised,' Sam the Lion said, 'that you had the nerve to come in this morning after the beatin' you all took. Anybody ever tell you boys about blockin'? Or tacklin'?

"Two of Crowell's four touchdowns had been run over Sonny's guard position, but he felt quite calm about it all. Four years of playing for Thalia had inured him to defeat."

— *from The Last Picture Show,*
a novel by Larry McMurtry

THE FOOTBALL TEAM
THAT NEVER WINS

I drove south on Interstate 81 at a pace which acknowledged the fact that I was not expected to arrive at my destination until the following day. I had weaseled some expense money from a magazine editor, my deadline was still comfortably in the future and a layer of pearl-gray clouds had cooled the late summer heat. It was, in all respects, a good day to be driving.

As one travels south beyond Waco the countryside changes sharply from mesquite-dotted flatland to gentle rolling hills and neatly laid out blackland farms. Were it not for the strategically placed franchise restaurants which serve up bad coffee, pass out free paper hats to the kiddies and peddle such items as ash trays shaped like the state of Texas, one could easily imagine himself driving through a time twenty years past.

Fifteen miles outside of Austin, I turned off the main highway. On a whim I had decided to pay a sentimental visit to Pflugerville, a community of 400 people, mostly German descendants, to look at a billboard the townspeople had erected in 1963.

There, as Farm-to-Market 685 runs past the high school, it stood, slightly worse for wear from the elements, but standing nonetheless. "Pflugerville," it read, "Home of the National High School Football Champions — 55 Straight Wins."

It had been October of 1962 when, so desperately in need of a passing grade in Feature Writing 301, I cut all my Friday classes and took leave of the University of Texas to spend Game Day in Pflugerville.

It was a setting tailor-made, a drama waiting to be acted out by teen-age heroes who just the week before had won their forty-ninth consecutive game in a string which dated back to 1957. That victory had earned the Pflugerville High School Panthers a share of the national record set by Abilene High, a Class AAAA Texas powerhouse whose enrollment was three times that of the entire Pflugerville population.

Throughout the day I wandered through town, talking with resident boosters, taking the journalistic liberty of identifying myself as a representative of the *Dallas Morning News* (which I wasn't) rather than a slightly bewildered college sophomore (which I was) hoping to dazzle his professor with a feature article which would earn its author some measure of academic salvation. I shared a car fender with Joe Pfluger, a descendant of the town's founding father, listening as he recalled a night fifteen years previous when the Panthers had seen a thirty-game winning streak snapped by the troublesome Hutto Hippos. Hutto, as fate would have it, was the very team against which Pflugerville would attempt to break the record that night. "N' let me tell ya," he said, "our boys are out for just some of that revenge."

I could only wonder at the longevity record for grudge-keeping.

During my appointed rounds I was to learn that there were forty boys enrolled in Class B Pflugerville High and all but nine were members in good standing of the Panther football team. Seven, I was told, were scholastically ineligible, one served as waterboy and, Heaven forbid, there was one whose fate it was to sit with all those girls in study hall every afternoon while practice was in full stride. Sitting in Doris Lively's Cafe, I was briefed on this none-too-minor town scandal: "His momma jes' won't let him play," a coffee-drinking informer told me. "Hell, we all think it's plumb terrible but, let me tell you right here and now, she's one stubborn kind of woman."

Taking his advice, I turned my back on the reporter's responsibility to get both sides to the story and decided not to seek out Mrs. Stubborn Woman for her comment.

One had to ask precious few questions to learn that 30-year-old Charles Kuempel was regarded locally as something of a coaching genius despite the fact he had never played all that much football during his younger days.

And there was much excitement over the rumor that Texas A&M had promised 17-year-old quarterback Joe Weiss, the 6-4, 200-pound star of the team, the moon if he would simply agree to play his college ball for the Aggies. There was, however, some concern over whether Joe's cousin, Willard Hebbe, a 135-pound slotback, would grow enough to rate much attention from college scouts. But, as Joe Pfluger had told me earlier, "in Pflugerville, size ain't all that counts." Case in point was reserve Panther lineman Danny Steger, a tiger who weighed in at 90 pounds soaking wet.

All had been playing tackle football since getting their parents' written approval to try out for the fourth grade team. And, to the man, they still could only wonder what it felt like to be on the losing end of a score.

The day dragged, noon slowly giving away to mid-afternoon, afternoon creeping toward the tension of game time.

Though the kick-off was scheduled for 7:30, an overflow crowd had gathered in old Fritz Pfluger's renovated cow pasture by six to assure itself a good view of history in the making.

After the teams had gone through their pre-game warmups, the Rev. Wilson Hill, pastor of the Immanuel Lutheran Church, and public address announcer at all Panther home games, delivered the invocation. It came as no great surprise to local residents that he ended his prayer saying, "Lord, we need this one tonight. We've just got to have it . . . "

I should here avoid the O. Henry urge and point out that they got it, with a couple of touchdowns to spare. Hutto made a valiant attempt to stop the repeated line bursts of Weiss but by late in the third quarter Pflugerville was coasting toward victory number fifty.

For the Panthers there would be five more wins, a write-up in *Time* magazine and a community-wide fund-raising to purchase a billboard before the streak would finally come to an end.

I passed slowly through town, by Doris Lively's Cafe and out toward the stadium, wondering what had become of those young boys who, for a relatively brief period in time, had been part of something unique, had done something none before them had ever done. Had the Joe Weisses and Willard Hebbes and Danny Stegers, now ten years removed from the world of win streaks, letter jackets and pep rallies, managed to successfully negotiate passage into the work-a-day world?

It was a question which fascinated me; one, I thought, that might even form the foundation for another story someday hence. But it was Sunday and

30

the residents had deserted downtown in favor of the privacy of their homes so there was no one to talk to. It would have to wait.

And, too, there were still 300 miles stretching before me. In Asherton, Texas, but a stone's throw from the Mexican border, there was a different kind of story waiting.

The next morning I was to visit Coleman Bailey, the man who had coached Hutto on the night that Pflugerville had become the winningest schoolboy team in history. He was now the superintendent at Asherton High School where for longer than he cared to remember the Trojans had been referred to as . . .

The Football Team That Never Wins

It sits in the cheerless waste country of South Texas, just off U.S. Highway 83, claiming 1,645 people, a dry goods store, a paintless Spanish-speaking movie house which opens on Saturday nights, a feed and seed, and a half-dozen gas station-liquor stores vying for the trade which passes by heading south for Laredo or north to San Antonio.

Asherton is bordered by mesquite and scrub brush in a part of the world as barren as the Depression times which robbed the community of a bank, a railway station, and much hope for a better tomorrow.

There is little to distinguish it from such neighboring hamlets as Big Wells, Brundage or Carrizo Springs. Populated largely by Mexican-American migrant workers who board up their homes each summer to head north to the beet fields of Montana and Nebraska, it is a town with a depressingly low per capita income. It is not, however, the two-dollar woes of day-to-day living which command much of the conversation at the Tropical Inn coffee shop. Rather, it is the fate of the hometown Asherton High Trojans football team, a member of District 30-A, which would enter the 1972 season with a losing

31

streak which had now stretched to forty consecutive games.

The ignominious string of defeats ranks as the longest in the colorful history of Texas schoolboy football. Thus in a state where the all-winning exploits of the Abilenes and Pflugervilles and Brownwoods are revered conversation pieces, the load of being the losingest of losers is a weighty burden to bear.

Though he practices his trade in a section of the country which often reveres high school football coaches over all other gifted craftsmen and pays them better to prove it, Terry Harlin, the 24-year-old head coach of the Trojans, receives only $600 of his annual $7,200 teaching salary for carrying out the duties of coaching football, basketball and baseball.

Prior to inheriting thirty of the team's losses when he accepted the Asherton job in 1971, the extent of his coaching experience was wrapped into the season he spent directing the 1970 Oklahoma School for the Deaf to a 5-5 season record. In his first year at the Asherton helm he exuded the brand of enthusiasm and confidence which has led local supporters to believe that the future promises more positive accomplishments from their young heroes. That he never played a single down of high school or college football, confining his modest athletic career to playing second base for Stonewall (Oklahoma) High, is of little concern to Trojan fans. Question his devotion to the game and half a dozen townspeople will point out the fact that he spent part of the summer taking a course titled "Fundamentals of Coaching Football" at West Texas State University.

"His ability to relate to the youngsters of the community," notes local priest, Father Francisco, "has already had a strong, worthwhile effect on the young people. Maybe he hasn't won any football games yet but he has won a great deal of respect from residents of the community."

Since Harlin's arrival, numerous signs of progress

have been noticed. When, for instance, nearby Carrizo Springs decided it would replace its old scoreboard, he asked for and was given their old one. Thus, the first electric scoreboard in Asherton High history now occupies a prominent place on the south end of the 500-seat Trojan Stadium. Several teachers on the faculty have volunteered whatever help they might lend and there is even talk among members of the high school board of raising funds to outfit a junior high team in the near future.

"There was," says Booster Club president Mariano Garcia, "a center on the 1962 Asherton team who is responsible for the only football trophy to be found in the school's trophy case, for 'great improvement last year'. The season before he came, the team didn't even score — not a point in ten games."

Last year the Trojans lost one by only 26-20, another by 16-8, and allowed no more than 48 points to any single opponent.

Harlin insists that despite the special problems related to his job he approaches his duties in the same manner of any other schoolboy coach one might find dedicated to molding young lives and winning championships.

"I'd have to say I'm fairly tough on the kids," he says. "Since we have no junior high or B-team, our players step right into varsity competition with little or no background in football. I do my best to prepare them as quickly as possible.

"We've got the same kind of training rules that everyone else does and the players are expected to adhere to them. If they don't they're dropped from the team. If someone misses practice without a legitimate excuse, he is dismissed. The players have accepted the rules, however, and I've had no discipline problems at all."

Harlin's methods, says team quarterback, Raul Gutierrez, who dreams of one day playing football for some college, are appreciated by the twenty-three-man Trojans squad. "He works hard and doesn't mind staying late to help us out," Raul says. "He's proved to us that he is interested. That's what we've been needing. Maybe with him coaching we can keep improving and win some games."

Time was when the Trojans sported the proud reputation of a hard-nosed, aggressive, winning football team. The "Mean Mexicans," rivals used to respectfully call them. There was the district championship in 1962, a near title in '65 and a 5-4 mark in '66. There has not been a winning campaign since.

In 1968 the team failed to win a single game and Ramiro Jamie, a graduate of Asherton High and for eight years its head coach, decided to end his career as Trojans coach and accepted a job at nearby Crystal City.

"I've been back to watch them play a few times," he says, "and it makes me sad. They try hard and they don't give up — you have to give them credit for that. You know, I'm a part of that losing streak. Ten games worth. When they break it, I'll celebrate right along with them."

Most of the youngsters who don't go north with their families in the summer are employed by Asherton's government-sponsored Neighborhood Youth Corps, a program which allows them to work at odd jobs for the city and school twenty-six hours per week for $1.60 an hour.

"Those who stay here," says the young Gutierrez who helps his father run the B&G Grocery, "stay in shape in the summer. We get together and run along the country roads or meet at the stadium and throw the ball around. It's hard to do much, though, since so many of the guys don't get back home until just before school starts.

"People come out to the games," he says, "but after we lose a couple they begin to get frustrated. They try to kid you about being a loser — you know, act like it's all a big joke — but you know they really mean what they're saying. I can't really blame them."

When Asherton High janitor Paulo Martinez drives the yellow school bus full of Trojans to such battlegrounds as Bracketville, Natalia and Mirando City, he transports them to an athletic world they are not familiar with.

"We go into the dressing room at another school," says tackle Fred Garcia, "and see all the equipment they have; the blocking dummies, projectors, rubdown tables and things like that. Sometimes it makes you stop and wonder if the losing streak is all our fault."

At Asherton there is no movie projector with stop-action button for review of game films. There are, for that matter, no game films taken. Nor can coach Harlin afford the luxury of scouting upcoming opponents. There are no funds set aside for things like stocking a modern training room or purchasing such practice aids as blocking dummies. Such has been the economic strain that last year was the first time in three years that school officials were able to present letter jackets to the graduating senior players.

"There is no question," says superintendent Coleman Bailey, himself a veteran of thirteen years of high school coaching, "that fielding a football team puts a financial burden on our budget, but we feel it is a vital part of the overall school program. Coach Harlin is doing a good job and is enthusiastic about what he's doing. He was offered another job last summer but chose to stay here and see that we break the losing streak. His dedication has begun to rub off on the kids and the community."

As is the case in most rural Texas towns the size of Asherton, high school football games provide the chief source of fall entertainment. Therefore, one can count on most of the elder residents to join the 123-member student body in cheering the maroon and white-clad Trojans to a hoped for victory.

"The football program," says Harlin, "is important to a community like ours. There's not much else to do in town so the football team gives people something to talk about

35

during the week and someplace to go on the weekends.

"And, I'd like to think that despite the fact we haven't had much success lately there is something that the kids get out of being a part of the team. (Joy did come to Asherton the previous winter when the basketball team defeated Eden, 32-20, thus ending a 62-game losing string in that sport. Then the baseball team ended its spring season with a 9-6 won-lost record.) Playing football helps them to grow up, to accept responsibility. But, I'd like for this year's bunch of kids to graduate with some happy memories to reflect on when they get older. That's why we've got to win some this year."

Thus, as the new season approaches, the Asherton cheerleaders are practicing yells, planning pep rallies, and painting signs which urge the team to "Stomp the Bulldogs" and "Win No. 1." Mariano Garcia is already contacting members of the Trojans Booster Club, urging them to help in a ticket drive to assure a full house when the team opens the season in September. Harlin, eager for the campaign to begin, points to the fact that there are eight starters returning from last year's squad.

In Asherton, where there is little else, hope springs eternal. They like to think that maybe — just maybe — this will be the year they'll win one.

Proving once again that there is that section of our society which holds a special feeling for the underdog, people throughout the country took the plight of the Asherton Trojans to heart.

A sporting goods company was among the first to react, donating a blocking sled. Another sent along reconditioned shoulder pads and helmets. A Boston television talk show host had Terry Harlin as his guest and a Pennsylvania radio station adopted the Trojans, asking Harlin to call collect each week with his score so they might be the first to advise their listeners when the losing streak ended. A Houston television station dispatched a film crew to Asherton to do a special.

Mail postmarked from sea to shining sea arrived at Asherton High, urging Harlin and his Trojans to continue the battle. Many contained small donations to go along with their words of encouragement.

The students of Pittsburgh Holy Innocents Grade School wrote to say they were adopting the Trojans as their team as did the inmates of the Atlanta (Georgia) Federal Penitentiary. A deputy sheriff in Kansas wrote, saying he had worked in athletics before going into law enforcement and would be happy to send along his playbook and offered himself in the capacity of mail-order assistant coach. A recent college graduate from Oakland, California, applied for a job as an assistant, stating all he would expect in return was room and board. A similar application arrived the same day from Syracuse, New York.

A member of the Brevard (North Carolina) High School Blue Devils wrote, pointing out that the team on which he played had been 21-2 over the past two years and he hoped the enclosed plays he had diagrammed might be of some help. A San Diego reader sent a check for ten dollars, specifying the money be used to purchase tickets to a Trojans game for grade school boys who would "one day grow up to become proud members of the Asherton team." A woman from Jefferson City, Missouri, reflecting on a mother-eye view of that school's national winning streak record, suggested that perhaps players at Asherton High might well stand to benefit more from their hardships. Almost without exception each letter asked that Harlin let them know when he and his Trojans broke into the win column.

The story appeared in the September third edition of *Parade,* a national Sunday newspaper supplement carried by over 100 papers. Five days later the Trojans opened the 1972 season by defeating the Crystal City 'B' team, 12-6. There was much celebrating, tears, and Harlin, a winner at last, was carried off the field atop the shoulders of his conquering heroes.

English students were assigned the happy duty of

37

writing letters to spread the good news to such far-flung places as Hanford, California, Fairfax, Indiana, and Peaks Island, Maine.

On the eve of his district opener Harlin, overseeing a team which was by then 4-2, called to tell me of the effect the piece had had on the community. There were, he reported, a total of 43 boys out for the team, enabling the Trojans to field a 'B' team as well as a varsity squad for the first time in the school's history. "The spirit around school," he said, "is really something. The kids, the other teachers — everyone has really gotten involved in the program. We've even got quite a few people following us on out-of-town trips now.

"And the really great thing is that the kids are thinking they can win every time we step on the field."

While the enthusiasm never waned, the caliber of opposition grew stronger in league play. A note from Harlin arrived at the season's end, stating that they had lost their last four and wound up the year with a 4-6 record.

It was, in the style of every coach I have ever known, a letter filled with disappointment over the fact the team had not won more. "But," he concluded, "we took some big steps in the right direction this season. Next year we should be able to really get with them."

Thinking that what my friends had come to call the Saga of Asherton High was over, I replied to Harlin's note, congratulating him on the season, thanking him for sending the letters he had received and wishing him well as he switched from football to basketball.

There would, however, be a post script to the story.

A few days after mailing the letter to Harlin I received a long distance call which a young lady on the other end of the line told me was coming from the Department of Justice in Washington, D.C. I swallowed hard, wondered what dastardly deed I had been accused of and admitted that, yes, I was the same Carlton Stowers whose byline had appeared on the *Parade* article.

A few seconds later, Gil Pompa, assistant director of

community relations, was on the line, explaining that the duty of his department was to lend a hand to minority communities in need of help.

"I recently received a call from Senator John Tunney of California," he explained. "He had read your story on the football team in Asherton, Texas, and suggested maybe we could be of some help to the school down there. What do you think about our seeing if we can't raise some money to help buy them some athletic equipment or something?"

Doing my best to sound as if I got a call from the Department of Justice every day telling me that Senator So-and-So had read something I wrote, I said I thought it would be a very worthwhile and much appreciated gesture.

"Here's what we've got in mind," he said. "I've contacted Joe Kapp, the former Minnesota Vikings quarterback, and Ken Aspromonte, the manager of the Cleveland Indians, and they both have agreed to come down there for a few days and see what they can do to raise some money for the high school.

"Now, the reason I called is to invite you to come along."

There was no great amount of time needed to make a decision, thus the following week I flew into San Antonio where Kapp and Aspromonte met me at the airport.

Both were members of a newly formed government program called STAR (Supportive Talents Assistance Resources). Its purpose is to utilize the donated time and efforts of celebrities to assist minority communities and groups through such fund-raising activities as telethons, benefits and guest appearances at school assemblies and community gatherings.

"We talked with Pompa," said Aspromonte, "and since there is very little money in Asherton, we've planned a few things in cities in the general area." There had been a dinner and reception the night before in San Antonio

39

and our route from the airport would take us to Eagle Pass, Crystal City and, finally, Asherton.

Advised of the heavy concentration of Mexican-Americans in the region, Aspromonte, the newly appointed coordinator of STAR, suggested that the colorful Kapp, a man ofttimes referred to as "the toughest Chicano ever to play football," be the headliner of the two-man troupe.

At Eagle Pass the two spoke to a high school assembly before a downtown luncheon with businessmen of the community. The chicken fried steak, green beans and visit with Kapp added a couple of hundred dollars to the Asherton Fund.

From there Aspromonte, a Brooklyn-born Italian-American who kept wondering where all the tall buildings were, drove on to Crystal City where the high school students heard him and Kapp urged them to stay in school, set high goals for themselves, and be sure to remind their folks about the Joe Kapp Banquet scheduled for that night.

Next stop, Asherton.

On their arrival, Aspromonte and Kapp were met outside the school by members of the football team, each smiling broadly and shaking hands with the first honest-to-goodness sports celebrity they had ever seen.

Inside the school auditorium they spoke to an awed group of youngsters, signed autographs and received a standing ovation. Long after the final bell had signaled that school was over for the day the students remained, giggling, laughing and thoroughly enjoying the presence of these men who had found their way from Washington and San Francisco, respectively, to Asherton, Texas population 1,645.

In nearby Crystal City there was scheduled the final event of the trip, a banquet where for $1.50 per person, people could come to eat their fill of tamales, tacos, and refried beans and mingle with the visiting celebrities.

But first there was a stop at the hospital in Carizzo

Springs. Terry Harlin, Jr. had chosen 3:45 p.m. of that particular day to come into the world, preventing his father's being at the school assembly earlier. When word came that mom and son were safe and well, Kapp suggested that the new father might get a little color back if he accompanied us to a barbeque stand we had passed en route to the hospital.

There, they talked with him about his program and informed him that something in the neighborhood of $500 had been raised in the past few days.

"The money," said Harlin, "is a great, great thing. But even more important is the fact that two well-known, very busy men took time to come all the way down here to show our kids that there are other people aware of them, people who care about what they make of themselves. It has meant a great deal to everyone in Asherton and, believe me, it will be a long time before they stop talking about this."

*To the German-descended citizens of Pfluger-
ville, Texas (pop.: 400), the most important things in
life, in approximate order, are chores, church and
football.*

— Time Magazine

GREATNESS IS ENDURING

There has not been enough passage of time to properly determine if the fates of the Asherton High Trojans
have really changed for good. I do notice as I read the
Saturday morning football scores where they now win
occassionally and seldom are the defeats embarrassing
to the degree they once were. The town itself, however,
remains hard-scrabble poor, locked in a time capsule
kind of Depression from which it cannot escape.

Barring an act of God or the arrival of some benevo-
lent Arab sheik, it is not likely to ever hear even the most
muffled of booms. Two-dollar miseries were, are, and for-
ever will be the burden of the people of Asherton have to
bear.

State football championships are simply not molded
from such environment.

Pflugerville, on the other hand, continues to prosper,
even if its national record winning streak has been eclipsed
several times over since the Panthers finally lost what
would have been Number 56 to Holland in Bi-district
back in November of 1962.

Still, the town and the school have grown and much of the enthusiasm that was evident in the late '50s and '60s remains. Deep in the hearts of many long-time residents there remains that eternal hope that one day another streak, with all the attending hoopla and celebration, might just start. After all, they did it once.

Keeping a long-held promise to myself, I indulged in a bit of nostalgia recently, retracing my steps to determine what had in fact, happened to the winningest football team I'd ever seen play.

I was not as interested in the community, with its new housing additions and fast food restaurants, or the current edition of the Pflugerville High team as I was in seeing how time had treated those youngsters who had, at one time, collectively brought national fame to what was then just another of Texas' rural farming communities.

I wanted to learn if such fame is, as we're so often told, all that fleeting. Or if as I secretly hoped . . .

Greatness Is Enduring

The old newspaper clippings are yellowed and brittle now, seldom brought out to reflect upon but Joe Weiss, a project engineer for Texaco in Port Arthur, keeps them nonetheless. Someday, he says his grandkids might get a kick out of seeing them.

Glen Wieland, now living in Houston where he is a mechanical engineer for Armco Steel, maintains a vivid memory of those days and points out that his parents who run the auto supply shop back home faithfully clipped the newspapers and look upon a leather-bound scrapbook as one of their prized possessions. Willard Hebbe, a cousin of Weiss' who is a computer programmer for Lockheed in Houston, also has a scrapbook somewhere and still delights in recalling the class reunion which was held a few years ago.

"You know," he says, "it was fun back then, being in high school and having a part in something that turned out to be a little special. Shoot, yes, I still get a kick out of thinking about it now and then, just remembering how at one time we had accomplished something nobody else had ever done before."

He is talking about the Pflugerville High School Panthers football team which, from the opening game of the 1958 season until a Friday the 13th bi-district battle with Holland in November of 1962, was never defeated. The Class B Panthers won 55 consecutive games, breaking the national winning streak record of 49 held previously by Class AAAA Abilene High School. During that incredible span the Panthers scored 2,354 points while holding their opponents to only 251. Thirty of their victories were shutouts. Johnson City's 21 points were the most ever scored on a group of youngsters who had gone through junior high and high school without every having to deal with defeat until Holland scored a 12-6 win which brought the dream to an end.

Fifteen years, it would seem, have done little to dim the memories of those closely associated with the Panthers in that time when they so methodically went about accomplishing what no 16- and 17-year-old boys before them had ever managed. Few days go by that the glories of the late '50s and early '60s are not resurrected for the benefit of a stranger passing through or to pass away the time between a couple of Lone Stars down at Knebel's Tavern. In the minds of many long time Pflugerville residents, the Joe Weisses and Willard Hebbes and Glen Wielands are still 17 years old.

George Pfluger, proprietor of the local barbecue establishment and descendant of the community's founding father, needs only slight prodding to drift back to those autumn Friday nights before the town began to experience a population growth brought on by nearby Austin people moving in; a time when everyone knew everyone and the Panthers' games brought everything in town to a standstill.

"Most folks," he says, "remember the night we broke the record (defeating Hutto 30-6) or the night over in Tay-

44

lor when Holland whipped us." Pfluger, however, points to the 21st victory in the streak, a last minute 13-12 win over Johnson City, as the one he most fondly recalls.

"They had a bunch of big ol' boys, a lot bigger than our kids," he says, "I think they had something like 45 players on their varsity along — that was more boys than we had in our whole school system — and by all rights probably should have beaten us by a couple of touchdowns. In fact, they outplayed us most of the night. But we stayed in it and late in the game Willard (Hebbe) gets behind a defender and makes an unbelievable catch for a touchdown that wins the game for us. Boy, he was a money player.

"That's the game that convinced me that bunch of kids were something special. If we hadn't won that one, of course, there would have been no national record to talk about, no sign put up on the highway by the booster club saying we were the best in the country, I guarantee you that much. But after we won that one, nobody else ever came close. Those kids had it set in their minds that they could whip anybody."

H. L. (Hub) Kuempel, an assistant coach during the Pflugerville glory days and the closest thing to an official historian of the record setting days, sits in his small office at the elementary school where he now serves as principal, flipping through scores of each game and producing a list which includes the name of each player who had a part in the Panthers' 55-game streak. He is also custodian of the badly worn game film taken the night they broke the old record against Hutto.

"Our budget didn't allow for the filming of every game," he explains, "but we got enough money together to film that one. We still get it out every now and then and look at it. Not too often anymore, though. It's about worn out."

Charles Kuempel, now retired from his head coaching duties to farm and ranch outside of the community where he and his young legions were once the toast of

45

the town, holds fond memories for those days of glory.

"That," he says, "was as fine a group of boys as you could ever hope to get together. And, yes we had some outstanding athletes in the bunch. Weiss was 6-3 and weighed 200 pounds; that's not bad for a Class B quarterback, and he went to Texas A&M and did a good job. And E. H. Emken, our end and punter, was 6-0 and 190 and went on to play ball at Southwest Texas State. But it was a team thing, from the first win to the last. We had a freshman lineman named Danny Steger who got in a lot of games for us the year we broke the record and he didn't weigh but something like 92 pounds."

"Football was important," he continues, "but I honestly don't think we ever let it get out of hand. On Sunday mornings the 16 boys we had on the varsity would all sit together at the Lutheran church. They were involved in other activities at school — FFA, 4-H, things like that. And we didn't spend all that much time on the practice field. All our boys lived out on farms, so we would get out at 2:15 for practice and everyone would have to be showered and ready to ride the bus home at 3:30. That didn't really give us much time. What it amounted to was that a lot of our practice came in the games themselves."

What they might have lacked in practice time, they made up for with togetherness. In 1962, in fact, the roster sounded much like a family reunion. There were the three Hodde brothers — Harvey, Vernon and Calvin; the Bohls brothers, Lanier and Treldon; the Hebbes, Willard and Lloyd, who were cousins of Weiss. Danny and Bobby Kreuger were nephews of Coach Hub Kuempel. And the two coaches were second cousins.

"Those boys," says grocery store owner J. B. Marshall, whose son J. B., Jr., now an attorney in Pflugerville, played in the first 30 victories of the streak, "accomplished a great deal, something they'll never forget. None of us will. They gave us all something to remember. And, what's even more important, it didn't stop

46

when they got out of school. They've all gone into the world and done pretty well for themselves."

Indeed, a check on who is where now fails to reveal any stories of defeat. The Pflugerville Panthers, now 15 years older, are still winning. They are college professors, restaurant managers, engineers, postal workers, farmers, veterinarians and electricians.

One, James Bohls, a 1962 graduate who had a part in 45 of the 55 victories, even returned to coach his alma mater for a couple of years after Kuempel resigned. He had been coaching at Hondo, fresh from a district championship, when he returned to Pflugerville for the Christmas holidays and visited with his former coach.

"He told me then that he was thinking about retiring and urged me to apply for the job. I don't think I ever would have if he hadn't brought it up first. I just couldn't imagine trying to take his place.

"He made football fun. Oh, we worked hard when we were out there but he never made any outrageous demands. And he was a good friend to everyone on the team. I would never have gotten a scholarship to Texas Lutheran if he hadn't put in a good word for me," says Bohls.

Bohls coached the Panthers for a couple of years with minimal success and then left the coaching ranks for fulltime teaching duties at PHS. It has been a nice homecoming since his parents live in Pflugerville and his wife's parents are a few miles away in Hutto.

Austin restaurant manager, Luther Watson, once a Panther guard, recalls there was rarely a lot of stone-faced seriousness to be found on the team. "In fact, we were probably the loosest football team you've ever seen. We had fun. Until it came time for the kickoff, then we got down to business."

He recalls the afternoon the entire school population assembled in the high school gym to watch a television program called "To Tell The Truth" on which their coach was going to appear. It was after the record had been set.

"They showed Coach in silhouette behind this screen and as soon as they did, E.H. (Emken) stood up and yelled, "There's Coach. You can recognize the way his ears stick out." That brought the house down.

"Yeah, keeping the streak going was important and fun, but there were other things, too."

A check of the Pflugerville High annual verified his statement. Tackle C.J. King, now a postal worker in Austin, was also the district literary winner in his senior year. Weiss was the senior class president, presided over the National Honor Society and ended his academic career with a record that just might be even more incredible than the one set by the footballers. In 12 years he never missed a single day of class. Willard Hebbe, wingback, was the senior vice president, and tackle Kenneth Schmidt, who went on to get his veterinarian degree at A&M, was president of the National Beta Club. Guard Jimmy Mott was sports editor of the yearbook.

Coach Charles Kuempel has made it a point to keep up with as many of the players he coached during the 19-year tenure as possible. Those who helped to set the record, he especially watches over. He can quickly and with obvious pride tell you what many of them are doing today.

"Several of them are still around here, farming," he says. "Anton Schoenrock, our center, is living over at Hutto on a nice little place he has. Harvey Hodde is farming just outside of town. Jimmy Mott still lives out here and works for the telephone company in Austin. Eddie Tyler is now a chemical engineer in Port Arthur, and Glenn Weiss, Joe's older brother, is a supervisor for Texaco out in El Paso. Ralph Engleman, an end, is a vet over in Arkansas. Charles Collier, a sophomore running back for us when we set the record, is an electrician in Austin, and Ed Bohls, James' brother, is a dental technician in San Antonio. Steve Doerfler, one of our guards, is working for a refinery over in Baton Rouge, and Kenneth Johnson, another good lineman, is ranching and in the real estate business in Austin. Bobby Kruger has a dairy over at Hutto and Treldon Bohls, who was our trainer, is working for the IRS in Austin. Lloyd Hebbe is down at the First State Bank here in town, and Calvin Hodde is a career military man. Charles Mott, now a radiologist in Austin, serves as the Pflugerville team doctor on Friday nights . . . ''

You get the idea.

They were, then, from a special time and place. Pflugerville was a little bitty town back then,'' says Joe Weiss. ''Everyone knew everyone and was interested in what the other fella was doing; interested in helping him. Everyone was hard working and I suppose it rubbed off on their kids. Most of us worked pretty hard at whatever we did. I think one of the reasons everyone seems to have done pretty well with their lives is the fact that we learned what hard work and determination could do. Coach Kuempel had a lot to do with that.''

Kuempel refuses to take the kind of credit his former quarterback seeks to hand him. ''Oh, I'd like to think as a coach I made my contribution, but it was the kids, the attitude of the town, a lot of little things, that went into what these men have done with their lives. Those kids weren't in school just to play football. They had goals, they wanted to make something of themselves.

''I guess,'' he continues, ''I was about as proud of them the night they finally lost as I was when they were winning. I often wondered how they would take it when the time came. I'll never forget the game. We just weren't able to do anything right. We had a pass dropped that was a sure touchdown, then had another touchdown called back. It was just one of those nights and still we just got beat by just six points.

''The kids came into the dressing room and sat quietly for a few minutes. There were no tears, no violent show of anger. We talked for a few minutes and then they all got up and went over to Holland's dressing room and congratulated the other team.''

49

He pulled an annual down from the shelf and flipped the pages, in search of something as he talked. "Pflugerville is a lot larger now. We've got over 1,000 kids in our school system. It's not like it was back when we were a little ol' Class B school in a little wide-spot-in-the-road town. But, the fact we were a little smaller and maybe didn't have much money for new uniforms and fancy equipment never bothered us.

"Here," he said, having found the page in the annual he had been seeking, "this says it all."

It was a quote by Adlai Stevenson which some astute yearbook editor had chosen to include in his publication. "Bigness," it read, "is imposing. But greatness is enduring."

The Pflugerville Panthers of 1958-1962 have endured.

"Ken Hall, you see, is the best high school football player ever. Period. Nobody else is even close..."
— *from Sports Illustrated*

THE SUGAR LAND EXPRESS

As a West Texas youngster first imagining the football glories that would one day be mine, I heard his name with no small measure of discomfort on several occasions. Kenneth Hall, playing for Sugar Land High School just south of Houston, was setting the kind of rushing records that caused suspicious brow-raising even among us 12-going-on-13 sandlot heroes generally ready to believe most anything.

The accomplishments of Hall, however, were among those I chose to disregard even if my dad and others down at the City Cafe swore them to be gospel. It was, frankly, the kind of competition I had no need for. After all, it was my own plan to run for celestial yardage once I arrived in high school, to earn All-This and All-That before sorting through the jillion or so college scholarship offers that were sure to come my way. Immodest though it might sound, I envisioned the day when there would be a statue of You Know Who erected down on the courthouse lawn. There it would be: a monument sculpted from stone, your author's likeness frozen in a stiff-arming pose as he averted yet another futile attempt by a would-be tackler en route to the game-winning touchdown. I dreamed big. But this guy Hall was beating me to the punch.

In more private moments I wondered if I would be able to match the records of this super-human who I never saw play. My best bet, I finally decided, was to simply view his achievements as folk tales originated by an over-zealous following of the Sugar Land Gators. The simple fact occurred to me that nobody, even if he was spending his Friday nights running against the Little Sisters of the Poor, could be that good. Seven touchdowns in a single game? Impossible. A guy who could run, pass and kick better than any other high schooler who ever played the game? Very unlikely. Still, the stories persisted. He was big, fast, strong, kind to his mother, gave all the credit to his lineman, played a mean trumpet in the band, got straight A's on his report card, and was voted Most Handsome, if you can believe it.

Which, as I've already mentioned, I chose not to. I held my ground for the better part of thirty years despite the fact his name and recollection of his heroics continued to come up from time to time.

While he had managed to become a full-blown Lone Star legend, I had done nothing more glamor-demanding than earn a letter jacket. The statue, I am forced to report, is yet to be built.

Recently, while thumbing through a national high school record book in search of some obscure statistic, I was a bit surprised to find his name. Not once, but several times. There, in black and white, was the proof I'd long avoided. In the years since he played his last game for the Class B Gators, Ken Hall's records had remained unchallenged.

It was time for me to fess up; to join forces with those who still regard him as the greatest high school football player in Texas history. But to do so I had to talk to him, to hear the stories first-hand. Why, I wondered, had he not gone on to collegiate greatness? What

52

had caused such great promise to burn out before Ken Hall's proper installation in the Pro Football Hall of Fame? What, in fact, had ever become of . . .

The Sugar Land Express

It sits at the far end of a tree-shaded street lined with the sweet, nostalgic scent of lantana and honeysuckle, looking newer now with its electronic scoreboard, additional seating and modern track which rings the football field, but the stadium is basically the same as it was 30 years ago when it was the focal point of the community's social activity.

Back then, in the early '50s, the 2,000 residents of this slow-paced, God-fearing town owed two loyalties; to the Imperial Sugar Company which paid everyone's salary and was the sole reason for the town being there in the first place, and the green-and-white Sugar Land High School Gators, a bonafide Class B football dynasty until consolidation shut it down in 1959 and caused students to be bussed up Highway 90 to attend John Foster Dulles in nearby Stafford.

Yet even as local elementary students now roam the halls of the white stucco building which was once the high school, memories of those glorious days past are kept alive by those who were there then, to see and cheer as their Gators captured regional championships and won 34 of 36 games during a three-year stretch.

Standing at the ticket window near the stadium's main entrance, his hands plunged deeply into his pockets, L. V. (Dugan) Hightower, retired coach of Sugar Land High, was clearly in a reflective mood. "People from all over came to see our games," he was saying. "Shoot, yes, they'd drive down from Houston, from over in Louisiana, all around. There were times when you could have filled a whole section with nothing but college coaches from all over the country.

"There would be so many people standing along the sidelines and in the back of the end zone that anytime

53

somebody scored or was run out of bounds, he just disappeared into a group of fans for a second or two.

"And you could always tell who the out-of-towners were. They would walk up to this window, buy their ticket, and ask the same question: 'What's *his* number?' "

Capacity in the stadium which now serves as the home field for local junior high games was just over 600 when it was the Friday night stage for a teen-age running back who was the talk of Texas. In a state where high school football has long been a six-point favorite over everything this side of Sunday-go-to-meetin', a 6-1, 205-pound tailback named Kenneth Hall, Number 31 for the hometown Gators, was something special. Those who were witness to his weekly feats stood four-square ready to favorably compare him to Chip Hilton multiplied by Jack Armstrong with any of the World's Seven Great Wonders thrown in for good measure. He dominated the game in a manner no schoolboy back had ever done before or has since.

Today, 29 years removed from that final game against Magnolia High team led by future Rice All-America and professional great Buddy Dial, Hall's name is still scattered throughout the national high school record book.

From 1950 through 1953, he went to the top of the schoolboy rankings in a dozen categories and still holds the marks in eleven: Most points scored in a career (899) and a season (395), most touchdowns in a career (127) and a season (57), most total yards in a career (14,558) and a season (5,146), most total yards per game average (428.8), most rushing yards in a career (11,232) and a season (4,045) and average per game (337.1), most 100-yard games in a career (38) and most consecutive 100-yard games (21).

He also kicked 137 extra points and passed for 3,326 yards during his four-year statistical binge.

His 520 yards rushing in a single game in his senior year stood as the record until 1974 when John Bunch of

Elkins, Arizona rushed for 608. Bunch's record performance, it is worth noting, came on 38 carries in a game which saw him playing until the final gun. Hall, on the other hand, accomplished his 520 yards (and seven touchdowns) on just 11 carries — that's a 47.3 yards-per-carry average — and retired to the bench at the half.

When he wasn't breaking for long distance runs from scrimmage, he was adding to his total yardage with a 64-yard kickoff return, an 82-yard punt return, and a 21-yard return with an interception. By the time the Gators had claimed their 73-14 victory over an outclassed Houston Lutheran, Hall had amassed 687 total yards in just two quarters of play.

The following morning, trumpet in tow, he joined fellow members of the Sugar Land High band as it traveled to Austin for a marching contest. Football, clearly, was not Kenneth Hall's sole purpose in life.

Yet, so incredible are the marks he set that there is sound reason to doubt many of them will ever be broken. Over the last three decades the nation's media have celebrated the accomplishments of a lengthy parade of high school superstars, players like Tony Dorsett, Herschel Walker, Mickey Cureton, Billy Sims, David Overstreet and Marcus DuPree. And while their statistics were enough to make college recruiters slack-jawed, none managed to seriously challenge the standards set by Hall.

His career rushing total, for instance, is 3,494 yards better than second place Sims who managed an awesome 7,738 yards in his schoolboy career at Hooks (Tex.) High. In total offense, runnerup Ron Cuccia of Los Angeles Wilson High fell 3,107 yards shy of Hall's mark when he graduated in 1977.

And Coach Hightower adds a foreboding footnote: "There's no telling how many points he would have scored or yards he would have gained had we let him play the whole game against some of our weaker opponents. We had to take him out to keep from humiliating some of the schools we played."

Rice assistant coach Bobby Williams, who played against Hall while a schoolboy at rival Missouri City, calls him the greatest high school football player he's ever seen. "I've seen a lot of outstanding high school backs," he says, "but none I would even put in Hall's league. You had to have seen him to believe the things he did. I graduated a year ahead of him and went to Wharton Junior College, but I went to Sugar Land several times my freshman year just to see him play. He could run, pass, catch, punt, kick — what he was, was a big Doak Walker with 9.7 speed."

Those talents enabled Hall and his teammates to win 34, tie one and lose one in his final three years of high school. "We managed to tie them 12-12," recalls Williams, "by using a nine-man line the entire game. Kenneth still broke for two long touchdown runs, though." The lone defeat came when Hall, having suffered a neck injury the week before, was unable to play.

"There are people quick to assume that Kenneth's records were made against a lot of inferior teams," Hightower says, "but that was hardly the case. In all honesty, I'd have to say that our competition ranged from very poor to very good; not much different from what you find in high school ball today. Some of the teams we beat pretty badly were good ball clubs. Kenneth was the difference."

The Gators, with but 17 players on their roster, were running a single wing offense in a time when the T-formation was favored throughout most of the country. "People we would play hadn't seen our kind of offense — what it was was the Notre Dame Box — so it made it much harder to defense. We had Kenneth as the deep back, the tailback, taking the snap on every play . . . "

A smile spreads across his face as he reflects. He has remembered another story. "We were playing Orchard High one night — a pretty good football team — and they scored on us first, moving the ball right down the field. Then they kicked off and we got the ball on our own 20.

Kenneth called this sweep to the right and went 80 yards for a touchdown on our first play from scrimmage. But we were off-sides and were penalized five yards. So, he calls the same play to the left side and goes 85 for a touchdown.

"Just as soon as he scored, I noticed one of the officials calling time out. I assumed someone was hurt, so I ran out onto the field. I checked all of my kids and didn't see anyone down, then looked to see if any of the Orchard players were hurt. Everybody looked fine. Finally, I went over to the official and asked him what the time out was for. He looked up at me and said, 'I called it for me, dammit. That No. 31 of yours is running us to death.' "

Now Hightower was on a roll, the stories quickly coming to mind. "That night he set the single game scoring record against Houston Lutheran," he says, "was something. Granted, they were a weak team, but even against someone like that you don't expect to run and down the field the way Kenneth did.

"Chuzzy Jenkins was the head coach then — I was his assistant — and he knew that a kid named Dickie Todd from Crowell held the record. He'd scored 48 points in a game back in 1934. So, when Kenneth scored his seventh touchdown and tied the record, Chuzzy told him to go back in, kick the extra point to get the record, and then he would be through for the night.

"Neither of us could believe it when the team came out in scrimmage formation and Kenneth ran the ball in for the conversion. When he came off the field, I asked him why he hadn't kicked it. He didn't crack a smile, just said, 'Coach, I just wanted to be sure I made it and broke the record Coach Jenkins has been talking so much about, so I decided to run."

It was, Hightower emphasizes, hardly a matter of Hall's lacking confidence in his kicking abilities. Rather, it was a dramatic example of his confidence as a runner.

Such are the cornerstones upon which the legend of

Kenneth Hall, Super All-State and Wigwam Weisman Prep All-America pick, is built.

Today, when the performances and promise of gifted high school running backs are discussed, one can still count on his name coming into the conversation. Now living in Los Angeles in a fashionable suburban neighborhood populated by friends who have no idea he even played high school football, much less established unbelievable records, he is still the back all other schoolboys are measured against.

While his name is no longer familiar to many of today's new-breed fans who are concerned only with those achievements which rate mention in the morning's sports section, those who carefully guard the lore of high school football remember him well.

At age 45, Kenneth Hall remains one of their blue chip heroes.

Now vice-president for the Sweetner Products Company, Hall was sitting in his downtown Los Angeles office recently, questioning the interest in something he did 30 years ago. He is not, quite obviously, a man who lives in the past.

Thumbing through a high school record book he was seeing for the first time, he seemed genuinely surprised to see his name mentioned so often. "I can't believe the records haven't been broken. One of these days they will be, I'm sure. Frankly, I wasn't aware they kept so many records on high school ball. Back when I was playing, I only remember hearing about two records, the state record for most points in a season and a single game. My coach had done some research and found out what they were and told me about them when I was getting close to breaking them.

"But we never talked about any of the others, like yardage and total offense and all. And nobody ever thought about what the national records might be. That wasn't the purpose of playing the game, anyway. The big thing for us was to try to win the District 7-B championship. We just had a lot of fun. We had a very close-knit group of people on our team and everyone was willing to help the other guy. It was the winning that was fun, not the statistics."

If that hints of false modesty, be assured Kenneth Hall is not a man given to such pretense. He appears almost as shy today as he was in high school. The boy voted Most Handsome and Senior Class President and captain of the football team did not, obviously, gain such honors by great amounts of personal horn-blowing.

"You know, there was a time when I didn't like football at all. Never had the slightest intention of playing it. I was a frail kid when I was little and would go to almost any length to avoid getting hit. I didn't like to fight, didn't like contact of any kind. I was perfectly content to let the other guys play football while I practiced my trumpet and marched in the band.

"But in the eighth grade I decided to come out for football, just to give it a try. And found out quickly that I had made a big mistake. I do remember scoring a touchdown on about a 60-yard punt return that year, but that didn't really excite me too much. I just didn't enjoy playing."

Which was fine with Curtis and Imogene Hall. Neither had ever pushed their son in the direction of competitive athletics. "Dad had been a pretty good town baseball player in his younger days," Kenneth says, "but he had to quit school and go to work after completing the fourth grade, so he didn't know much about football. And Mom was just worried that I would get hurt. So there was no need for apology at home when I decided I didn't want to play anymore."

Even the fact he gained 50 pounds and six inches in height in the summer between his eighth grade and freshman year did not encourage him to give second thoughts to checking out a uniform. On the other hand, Head Coach H. L. (Chuzzy) Jenkins, in need of additional players for his high school squad, repeatedly urged the

59

young town constable's son to join the team.

Pressure, in due time, would be brought to bear. After the struggling Gators had lost their first five games of the 1950 season, Superintendent W. E. White, himself a former coach, called the 12 male members of the freshman class into the school auditorium and carefully explained the dire situation and need for volunteers. "He was," Hall remembers, "pretty persuasive. He even began helping Coach Jenkins with workouts, suggesting a change from the T-formation offense to the single wing Notre Dame Box."

When the 185-pound Hall reported for practice the following afternoon he was immediately installed as the tailback. By the time the season ended four weeks later he had scored 58 points and Sugar Land had closed out the year with victory margins of 53-0, 39-7, 26-0 and 13-0.

"In that last game of my freshman year — we were playing East Bernard — I scored the clinching touchdown on a 90-yard run. For some reason that touchdown meant a lot to me. From that point on, playing football became an enjoyable experience."

At one point in his sophomore season he had scored 70 of his team's first 102 points, an achievement which earned him a write-up in the nearby *Houston Post*. It would be the first of many. Before his high school playing days were over, the scrapbook his mother dutifully kept would include clippings from as far away as New York and several overseas papers.

"I was aware of the fact I was getting some national attention," he admits, "but it was never anything anyone made a big deal of. When you live in a small town with only about 100 kids in school — there were 24 in my graduating class — you really don't think too much about what's going on in the rest of the world, or stop to consider that it might be interested in what you're doing."

The pursuit of athletic records, in fact, was hardly the complete focus of Hall's young life. On Wednesdays, during his freshman and sophomore years, it was necessary for him to leave practice early so that he might get down to the Palms Theater where he worked as a door-man and usher. He continued to perform with the school band, showed considerable attention to a pretty class-mate named Gloria Ross, and tended his academic busi-ness well enough to graduate third in his class.

"A lot of things I remember about being in high school don't directly have to do with the games we played. For instance, one of the things that comes to mind was the fact that after every home game all the players were expected to report to the stadium to clean up the trash under the stands and around the concession area.

"And I can remember always taking Carlos Tarvor home with me on the afternoons before we had games. Mom would fix us a pre-game meal — a steak, toast, honey — while we sat out on the curb in front of the house and polished our football shoes."

Then, there were the gatherings at White's Cafe, where the Quarterback Club would foot the bill for chicken-fried steaks and cream gravy when the team re-turned from short-distance out-of-town games.

Which is to say the athletic lifestyle in Sugar Land was nothing more than typical of that found in most small Texas towns in the '50s. Being a member of the football team did, of course, provide one with a certain degree of stature in the community. "But," Hall insists, "none of us were ever put on a pedestal."

If he wasn't, there is legitimate reason to question the enthusiasm of his hometown sports fans.

In addition to his football heroics, Hall was a starter for the Gator basketball team and twice led Sugar Land to the state track and field championship, scoring 38 points in the state meet in his sophomore year and 36 in his junior year. He ran the 100 in 9.7, the 220 in 21.4, the 440 in 49 flat, long-jumped 23 feet, threw the shot 53 feet, handled the anchor leg on the 440-yard relay and oc-casionally threw the discus and high-jumped.

In his senior year, in fact, Superintendent White was

61

convinced that with the proper training Hall could represent the United States in the decathlon at the 1956 Olympic Games in Melbourne. "It was an idea that really fascinated me," Hall admits. "The only events I'd not done were the pole vault and the javelin and I felt I could learn them. Mr. White and I talked about it a great deal and I was excited about the possibility."

A hamstring injury suffered in the spring of his senior year not only put the decathlon dream on the back burner but also cost Sugar Land a third straight state title.

"He pulled the muscle at the Bay City Relays and was on crutches for a while," remembers Hightower, "but he got well enough toward the end of the season to qualify for the state meet again. When we got to Austin, we wrapped the leg good and thought he'd be okay. I remember before he was to run the 100, I told him to go over and take one of his throws in the shot put while he was still fresh. It wound up being the only throw he took and it stood up for second place. In the 100, he was leading by almost 10 yards when he pulled the muscle again and wasn't able to finish. That was it for him."

When Hall's records are recited, Hightower points out, one of the most impressive is always overlooked. "In four years, he scored 83 points in the state track meet. I don't think you're going to be able to find anyone who has ever come close to that."

The question which has been repeatedly asked of those who knew of his high school heroics is obvious: Whatever happened to Kenneth Hall? Why wasn't that golden promise fulfilled by college All-America accomplishments? Maybe even the Heisman. Or an Olympic gold medal. What caused high school football's most celebrated running back ever to all but disappear?

Eager recruiters had come to Sugar Land from throughout the country. The entire Notre Dame coaching staff had paid him a visit. Ohio State wanted him. So

62

did UCLA and Michigan and Arizona and Oklahoma and LSU. Coaches from every school in the Southwest Conference were greeted into the Hall home.

For most of his senior year an average of 60 letters a week arrived from coaches, pleading alumni and politicians, all suggesting that their favorite school would be ideal for him to attend and continue his athletic career.

From over 100 scholarship offers, Kenneth eventually decided on one extended by Bear Bryant at Texas A&M.

"I was aware of Bryant's success as a coach," Hall says, "and I liked the atmosphere and spirit I saw when I visited the A&M campus. I saw much of the same closeness I'd experienced at Sugar Land. And, too, it was relatively close to home."

Hall's decision came in a time before college recruiting had turned into a NCAA nightmare. There was pressure, he says, but never any offers that exceeded the standard four years of room, board, books, tuition and fees.

"I had made it clear to everyone that I wasn't interested in going out-of-state," he says, "so the schools in California and Arizona and places like that didn't stay in touch for long. It wasn't a real long, drawn-out affair."

Curtis Hall sought out the advice of the coaches and several townspeople, then instructed his son to carefully weigh his decision but make it as quickly as possible. Soon, Kenneth had narrowed his choices to Rice and A&M.

"When Coach Bryant came to visit my parents," Hall remembers, "the decision was pretty well made. Mom and Dad were very impressed with him. I can remember all of us sitting in the living room, talking, and after a while Coach Bryant invited my folks out to dinner. They talked for a few minutes more and then Mom turned to me and asked if I was going to get dressed. Coach Bryant looked at her, smiled, and said, 'He's not invited.'

"I was excited about playing for A&M and glad to have the decision behind me. While the pressures weren't as great back then as they seem to be now, it was good to have it over. That kind of thing is difficult for a 17-year-old kid to handle."

Not as difficult, however, as what was to come.

"When he reported for the first fall practice of his freshman year, Hall lined up at a halfback spot but was immediately moved over with the group of fullback hopefuls. That sudden switch, which had come with no advance warning, also dictated that he would be playing middle linebacker in the Aggies' one-platoon system.

"Suddenly," Hall recalls, "I was facing a lot of adjustments I hadn't anticipated. I had never done much blocking in high school and that was the primary duty of the fullback in Bryant's system. And, too, I'd never even been in a three-point stance before, having never played in the T-formation.

"Then, there was the matter of defense. That was my real drawback. I had played in the secondary my first three years in high school, then played some at linebacker as a senior. But I never enjoyed it. I would rather run over someone than have them running over me. In high school, because of my size, I had been able to make tackles without really delivering a punishing blow."

Still, when the freshman season opened with Hall at fullback and John David Crow and Ed Dudley at halfbacks, it was the powerful youngster from Sugar Land who was in the spotlight. The first time Kenneth Hall carried the ball as a collegian he ran for a touchdown. By season's end, he was the team's leading scorer.

Though not happy with the role of fullback, he was satisfied he had performed well in his first year of college. And as an added bonus he received a medal for being named the Outstanding Freshman Marching Cadet and had been successful as a member of the freshman track team.

But his abilities as a linebacker were the constant source of criticism from members of the coaching staff.

Midway through his sophomore year disenchantment began to weigh on him. "I worked hard," Hall says, "but I was sitting on the bench. Coach Bryant kept telling me I was going to be starting soon, but the time never came. After the seventh game of the season I decided I couldn't stand the situation any more and went home to Sugar Land and got married."

Fearing later that he had judged his situation too emotionally, Hall approached Bryant about returning for spring training that year, was accepted back, and immediately set about to challenge senior Jack Pardee for the starting fullback job.

His junior season, however, would be more of the same. Wearied of the practice session criticism he received and the spot duty he was dealt on game days, Hall again became discouraged. Still, he worked, hoping to convince Bryant and his assistants that he could contribute.

"Before we were to play Baylor midway through the season," he recalls, "I was told that I was going to start. Jack Pardee was injured and I was eager to get my chance. But just before the kickoff, Bryant told me he had decided to start Jack. I played some, gaining pretty good yardage every time I carried the ball, but just as soon as I felt I was really getting into the flow of the game, they would take me out. Before the game was over I found myself standing on the sidelines, wondering if I really wanted to play anymore.

"After the game I told Coach Bryant I was leaving. That was it; no discussion or anything. Maybe he just didn't think I could play. I don't know to this day. For some guys he was a father figure, but it was different for me. Things just didn't work out.

"I don't blame anyone. It was just one of those things in life you have to learn to deal with. Looking back, I'd have to say I learned something from the experience."

Ed Dudley, Hall's roommate at A&M, was one of the first to realize that the philosophical differences between Bryant and Hall were dooming a promising career. "We had a lot of long talks about it," he says. "Kenneth was one of those easy-going kind of kids who was never going to buck the system. Even when he was down and upset, I don't think it ever occurred to him to confront Bryant. If John David or I had had the same kind of problems he had, we'd have probably been kicking Coach Bryant's door in and demanding some kind of explanation, then maybe taken a punch at him. But that wasn't Kenneth's style. He would walk away from the situation before he ever did anything like that.

"I knew it wasn't going to work for him there at A&M and even went so far as to suggest he think about transferring to another school where he would get a chance to be the kind of football player I knew he was. That, or forget football and concentrate on the decathlon. There's no question in my mind that he could have made the Olympic team if he'd worked at it. He was that kind of athlete.

"I'm as great an admirer of Bear Bryant as any man who ever played for him," Dudley insists, "but he made a big mistake with Kenneth. In the first place, he should have never had him playing at fullback. He should have put John David at fullback and Hall at the halfback.

"That would have solved the defensive problem. In Bryant's scheme of things, the fullback automatically played linebacker while the halfbacks played in the secondary. With his speed and size, Kenneth could have done okay in the secondary. And John David could have done a good job at linebacker. But Bryant had his rules.

"It was a tragedy, really. Kenneth was such a gifted athlete. I saw him run a 9.9 100 in a pair of football shoes one afternoon. The problem was that he wasn't the kind of aggressive football player Bryant liked. Kenneth was never one who liked to hit someone for the sheer pleasure of hitting them. He realized it was a physical game, but I don't think he ever enjoyed that part of it.

"You know, when you first get to college, fresh out of high school, you're pretty confident of yourself, so you aren't really awed by the other freshmen athletes you come in contact with. That was my case until I met Ken-

neth Hall for the first time. I looked at him and thought, 'My God, am I going to have to try to beat this guy out for a job?' "

Crow remembers much the same reaction. "He looked like some kind of Greek god when he arrived. I was amazed by his size and speed. And he was a super person. We had some hot-shots on that freshman team who thought pretty highly of themselves, but Kenneth wasn't one of them.

"It's unfortunate that things didn't work out for him at A&M. It was just a personality thing between him and Coach Bryant. Back then Bryant felt you treated every one the same and that just didn't work. Me, I was one of those who needed a kick in the ass every now and then to get me going. Kenneth needed to be treated somewhat differently.

"Lord knows I love Coach Bryant to death, but I'll say this," the winner of the 1957 Heisman Trophy points out, "If Kenneth Hall had gone to play under someone like Bud Wilkinson at Oklahoma, the world would never have heard much about John David Crow."

When Hall left A&M for the second time, Crow went to Bryant and asked if the coach would like for him to go to Sugar Land and try to persuade Kenneth to return. "He said 'no'," Crow remembers, "so I let it drop.

"But to this day Coach Bryant regrets not having done something to keep Kenneth there. Just recently we were talking, in fact, and he told me, 'John David, you know if I'd let you go get Ken Hall when you asked me to, we would have won the national championship in '57.' I don't think there's any question about it."

In his autobiography, *Bear*, Bryant reflected on his handling of Hall:

"You have to learn what makes this or that Sammy run. For one it's a pat on the back, for another it's eating him out, for still another it's a fatherly talk or something else.

"You're a fool to think, as I did as a young coach, that you can treat them all alike. I know I've missed on a

67

lot of them. Ken Hall down at Texas A&M, for example
. . . My job was to get him to play, and I didn't. So
there's no doubt in my mind that I failed.

"I know this, if we had had Ken Hall in 1957 we
would have won the national championship. We were 166
points ahead in the polls with two games to go, and we
lost those, 7-6 to Rice and 9-7 to Texas. You don't think
Hall was worth three points to us?"

Imogene Hall was glad to see her son come home.
"Oh, I would have liked for him to have stayed and finished school there at A&M, but the situation had made
him a nervous wreck. It had begun to really get to him —
and to his father and me. He tried so hard that the frustration was just magnified. I could see what it was doing
to him.

"But neither his father nor I ever tried to intervene
in any way. Maybe that was the wrong decision, but I
was afraid I might say the wrong thing and just further
complicate his problems. The time came when he just
couldn't hack it any more. He gave it a good, honest try,
though. I'm proud of him for that."

Back home, Hall went to work for the Imperial
Sugar Company, uncertain of his future plans. "One day
late in the spring I got a call at work from Jim Owens,
one of the A&M assistant coaches who had taken the
head job at the University of Washington. He asked me
if I would be interested in coming up there and playing. I
told him I would and waited for him to get back in touch.
But, then, a couple of weeks later I got a telegram from
him saying he wouldn't be able to offer me a scholarship
because I'd only have one year of eligibility left. That, I
decided, was the end of my football career."

Enter Stu Clarkson, the former Chicago Bears guard
who had coached in the Canadian League before returning to Texas to take an assistant coaching position at
Sugar Land High. Stopping by the sugar company to see

Hall, he asked what his plans were and if he was still interested in playing football.

"I told him I didn't know for sure what I was going to do, but that I wasn't through playing football. I felt I had to prove — to Coach Bryant, I guess — that I could play. Stu asked if I had considered playing in Canada. I didn't even know it was a possibility, assuming they had the same rule against signing anyone whose college class hadn't graduated. He told me I could play up there right away if I was interested. I told him I was.

"He contacted Pop Ivy, who was coaching at Edmonton, and a few days later I got a call from him, saying he wanted to fly down and talk to me. He made me an offer and I agreed to be in Canada on the fifth of July to begin training camp."

While A&M was narrowly missing out on a national championship, Kenneth Hall was helping the Edmonton Eskimos to the semifinals of the Grey Cup playoffs, missing out on Rookie of the Year honors by a single vote. "We played a double fullback type backfield up there," he recalls, "and I was on the wing. I blocked, caught the ball, returned kickoffs and punts, everything. It was a great feeling to be playing again."

He would, during his year with the Eskimos, display much of the same ability fans back in Sugar Land had come to expect. Playing in a game against Calgary when the temperature was zero and his own fever registered 102, Hall rushed for 200 yards, returned a kickoff 100 yards, and scored three times.

When his graduating class became eligible for the 1958 NFL draft, he was selected in the fourteenth round by the Baltimore Colts and chose to take leave of Canada and prepare himself for the chance to play professional in the United States.

Though in competition with the likes of Lenny Moore and Alan Ameche, Hall was told by Coach Webb Ewbank on the eve of the final pre-season game that he had made the squad. The following day, however, fate and a linebacker named Sam Huff would deal Hall's hopes a serious blow.

"It was a freak thing, really," Hall recalls. "We were playing an exhibition in Louisville, Kentucky against the New York Giants and I was going up the middle on a simple dive play and I tripped over the guard. I went to one knee and was trying to get up when Huff hit me from behind. It bent me over and drove my head between my knees. The sixth vertebra in my neck just collapsed. It was cracked in five places.

"After that, I really never had all my coordination."

When the 1959 season began, Ewbank told Hall he had been traded to Pittsburgh, instructing him to report to Cardiff, Pennsylvania, where Buddy Parker's Steelers were training. "That was the strangest experience I had during my entire football career," Hall says. "I got there and practiced for three days but never got a playbook. I kept asking about it and kept getting put off. Finally, Parker told me that what they really needed were ends so he was making a deal for me with the Chicago Cardinals. The next thing I knew, I was on a plane to Seattle to their training camp."

The idea of joining the Cardinals appealed to Hall. Ivy, his Edmonton coach, had taken the Chicago job, and already on the roster were former A&M teammates Crow and Bobby Joe Conrad. "I liked the idea of being in the backfield with these guys. With King Hill of Rice at quarterback, we had an all-Southwest Conference backfield that year."

The reunion would last but a season as Hall was traded to the American Football League Houston Oilers in 1960, there to return kicks and share duties with Charlie Tolar in the backfield. For Kenneth and wife Gloria the trade represented a homecoming since they were able to return to live in Sugar Land, just a half hour's drive from Houston.

During that championship season, Hall found his way into the record books twice, setting a club mark for

70

the highest kickoff return average for a season — 31.2 yards on 19 returns — and accomplished a 104-yard return for a touchdown against the New York Jets.

The following year, however, a dislocated shoulder put him out of action and on the waiver list.

"That's when I decided I'd had enough," he says. "The sugar company had offered me a good job at home and it seemed like time to settle down and get on with a career. But, no sooner had I been waived, I got a call from John David. He said the Cardinals, who had moved to St. Louis by then, were in need of help at end and wanted to know if I could catch the ball. He asked if I could fly up and play the rest of the season. Conrad met me at the airport with a playbook and told me I would start the next Sunday. For the rest of that year he and I alternated at split end, carrying in plays.

"But that was it for me. The fun went out of it after the Oilers waived me. But, I managed to play five years of professional football and got a championship ring that year in Houston. I felt I had proved what I had set out to prove. I showed that I could play. Maybe I could have done it better but, still, I proved my point."

Indeed, there is material evidence that he did. Last fall, as Bear Bryant was nearing Amos Alonzo Stagg's record for career victories, a small article reflecting on Hall's brilliant high school career appeared. A clipping found its way to Bryant's attention.

"Out of the blue," Hall says, "I got this letter from him, telling me he was glad to see that I was successful in my business and all. In the letter he said he just wanted me to know that the biggest mistake he felt he'd made in his coaching career was the way he'd mishandled me when I was at A&M.

"I was really moved by the gesture. I wrote him back, wishing him luck against Auburn, and told him there were no hard feelings. I suggested to him that we were both young at the time. I hope he got a laugh out of that."

It was, Hall says, all a long time ago. Though still an

enthusiastic football fan, he deals little thought to his own playing days. His attention instead switched to the respective athletic careers of his two sons who are now grown and in college, and his professional climb which has seen him recently move to Los Angeles from San Francisco where he spent seven years as an executive with a sugar brokerage firm.

He plays a little golf, some tennis, takes evening walks with his wife, and seldom, if ever, thinks about those days when he was considered the greatest high school running back in the country.

"Really, it's all just a blur to me now," he says. "There comes a time when you put all those things behind you."

But not everyone has forgotten.

Dugan Hightower looked out onto the spring green turf of Sugar Land stadium and said, "It could have been a lot different for Kenneth. I was bitter toward Bear Bryant for a long time for the way he treated him. I don't think he ever got a chance up there at A&M. He told me as much. And it's a shame. He had so much potential.

"You know, when the high school here closed down, we had a lot of trophies and things they didn't want to move over to the new school, so I took them home with me. I've got some trophies we won in football and track and a few game films from when Kenneth was playing. I look at 'em now and then. And I've got his old game jersey. I wouldn't take anything for it."

With that he began walking toward the car, hurrying to beat a mid-afternoon rain which was beginning to fall. For a moment he stopped, turned, and shook his head.

"Yessir, he was something special. Lord, I'd give anything to see him out there on that field one more time."

We Midland High School Bulldogs played our well-attended football games on Friday nights; the George Washington Carver Hornets played on what we considered "our field" on Thursday or Saturday nights as it became available. Although our fifty-yard-line tickets went for all of a dollar-six-bits, you could watch the Hornets from the better seats for fifty cents.

We sometimes visited Carver games, swaggering in our purple and gold letter jackets, sure of our superiority as men and athletes. We laughed at the high-stepping antics of the Carver band . . . and were disappointed when the stands failed to erupt into multiple razor fights, as we had every confidence they would.

— from Confessions of a White Racist, by Larry L. King

THE LEGEND OF LIBERIA PARK

It is not my mission here to attempt to define the role of the black athlete in my home state. I could no better do that than I could unlock the secret miseries of the Mexican-American migrant workers in Asherton. I cannot, for the plain and simple reason that I have never walked one single mile in the shoes of a black man or a Mexican-American.

Thus I can only recite some of the things I have seen that might in some way mirror the status of black ath-

letes who have launched their careers within the boundaries of Texas.

It has, for years, been an almost accepted fact that
the outstanding black athletes, the 6-3, 250-pound lineman, the 9.4 sprinter, the 6-8 kid who averaged 18 re-
bounds a game, will make few headlines on the sports
pages of Texas newspapers after he gets to college. That,
for the simple reason that most Texas dailies deal the
bulk of their space to schools in the Southwest Conference rather than the Big Eight, Big Ten or Pacific Eight,
which is where you will find many Texas blacks competing.

If a gifted running back desired to continue to make
Texas his residence while playing college ball as recently
as ten years ago, he had the choice of a half dozen colleges
playing on the fringe of big time ball or could trip on down
to all-black Texas Southern or Prairie View A&M.

As late as 1969 many Texans pointed to the National Championship won by Darrell Royal's University
of Texas football team, boastfully advising the world
that the achievement of being voted No. 1 in both polls
had been accomplished without so much as one "nigger"
on the roster.

On the other hand, a favorite generalization for the
lackluster performance of SWC basketball teams when
they face intersectional foes has been that you simply
can't expect a bunch of good ol' white boys to be able to
go off to other parts of the free world and whip five
blacks in a game of basketball. One is led to believe that
the only task more impossible would be to put him in a
watermelon-eating contest with one of those kinky-
haired dudes.

There has been, however, a gradual move toward integration of athletic teams in the state; a trend pioneered
by Hayden Fry at Southern Methodist and Bill Yeoman
at the University of Houston. A milestone of sorts was
reached last fall when a powerful fullback named Roose-
velt Leaks led the University of Texas to the No. 3 spot
in the rankings and a Cotton Bowl victory over Ala-

bama. There are many who feel the last barrier has come tumbling for the simple reason that Texas, the state's leading institution, not only had a black running back, but one who was the star of the team to boot.

I doubt, however, that it will cause great charges of blacks to go rushing to Austin, begging scholarships.

For while the aforementioned Leaks was making All-Southwest Conference, Houston native Greg Pruitt was vying for the Heisman Trophy at Oklahoma, and Colorado's Charlie Davis, who had played on the West Columbia team Brownwood defeated in the state title game, was being named to various All-America teams.

Black Texas athletes have been too long welcomed at such campuses as UCLA, Michigan State, Wisconsin, Kansas, Colorado, Oklahoma and Missouri, just to name a few, to suddenly break out in the same kind of state pride that keeps all but precious few standout white high school stars south of the Red River.

"Well," one distinguished alumnus who prides himself in the amount of money he donates to the athletic fund of his favorite SWC school, says, "it's easy enough to explain, now isn't it? These blacks, they've been dirt poor all their lives, and when it comes time to get down to talking about somebody giving them something like an athletic scholarship, they got their hand out for a little bit more than the other kids. I've heard stories about them wanting new cars and clothes and a job where all they gotta do is go by once a week and pick up a paycheck.

"That's why they're going out-of-state to play ball. That, and the fact that the entrance exams are a little too tough at most of our schools."

I should say here that skin color is no property of a youngster who wants something more than books, room, board and tuition. And while I never darkened their classroom doors, I must assume that the academic requirements at, say, UCLA or Michigan State, rank right in there with "our schools."

And, lest you get the idea that it is only those cor-

75

rupt types up in the Midwest or out on the West Coast who don't mind paying a little extra for an athlete, let me recount the recruiting attempt one of the middle-sized Texas colleges made on a youngster still regarded as one of the state's best-ever running backs.

He had publicly stated that he would like nothing better than to be the first black to receive a scholarship to the University of Texas. His admission came, however, at a time in the state's athletic history when he might just as well have wished for Neil Armstrong's first step on the moon.

The fact that the state's major schools showed only token interest in him led a successful coach at the smaller school to assume he had a good shot at the prize young black.

He too assumed that he would have to compete dollar for dollar with the out-of-state schools bidding for the youngster's signature on a scholarship.

Thus he journeyed to the youngster's hometown and spent the day talking to various alumni from the school at which he was coaching. He talked with the assistant vice-president at the bank, the Chevrolet dealer, the man in the shoe store and an insurance salesman — all died-in-the-wool football fans eager to lend a hand.

He urged them to be at a reserved room in the best restaurant in town at 7 p.m. that evening.

That much accomplished, he paid a visit to the youngster's home and set about to tell him and his parents of the glories that would be his if he cast his lot with So-and-So College. In two hours' time he had not only described the strong Christian atmosphere which prevailed on his campus and assured the concerned parents that they took care of each boy like he was their own, but he also had the young athlete being drafted number one by the pros in just four short years and blessed with an education that would open Lord-knows-how-many doors when the time came to decide on a career.

That phase of the sales pitch accomplished and cer-

76

tain that mother and father were satisfactorily impressed with the offer Kind Coach from Our Home State had made, the visitor mentioned that there were a few men downtown who might be able to enlighten the boy about the courses of study they took and perhaps suggest a major the youngster might be interested in. "You folks get your hats on while we're gone and we'll be right back and take you out and buy you the biggest ol' steak in this town," he said.

Thus he hurriedly escorted the youngster to the restaurant where the town's leading businessmen were waiting.

"Son," the coach said, "you know all these gentlemen here — and certainly they know you. In fact, they want to show their appreciation to you for all the wonderful things you've been doing out on that football field for the past few years. You decide to throw in with us and these folks here, they're going to do some mighty nice things for you."

With that he began a rapid-fire whirl around the room. "You, Jake, what can you do for this fine young man down at the bank of yours if he comes to our school?"

"I could put $100 a month in a checking account for him."

And what about you Mr. Car Dealer?

"He'd look just fine riding around that campus you got down there in a new automobile."

Insurance Salesman?

"I happen to know for a fact nobody in his family has the proper amount of coverage. I can see that's taken care of."

Mr. Shoe Store Owner?

"No need for him to ever wear another hole in the bottom of his shoes before he comes by my place to get himself a new pair to his liking."

The youngster was flabbergasted, speechless.

"Now, son," the coach said, "no need for you to rush

77

this thing. You think it over for a while, talk to your folks about it if you have a mind to, and jes' let me know when the mood strikes you."

A few hours later, in the midst of a quiet dinner, the youngster surprised his parents, the visiting coach and, perhaps, himself, when he said, "Coach, I've made up my mind. I'm going to the West Coast school that's been talking to me."

It is generally acknowledged that he received no more or no less than what is allowable under the rules set by the NCAA, yet to this day the particular coach I have been describing will tell you that, yes, he was interested in the kid until he found out he had his hand out. "Then I backed off in a hurry. That sort of thing is just asking for trouble."

The athlete who was the centerpiece of his recruiting tale is now ten years removed from the incident, enjoying a comfortable living in professional football. "Tell the story in your book if you want to," he said, "but don't use any names or anything. It wouldn't do anyone any good for the names to come up.

"I don't get to Texas much any more," he continued, "except to play ball, but I understand things are getting better. I hope that's true."

I like to think it is. There are no longer any all-black schools like those King wrote about and such things as the Negro Schools State Championships are things of the past. Blacks are now playing with whites, making All-State, getting invitations to post-season all-star games and enjoying the same academic advantages as every other youngster living in their hometown.

Recruiters from Texas colleges now spend great amounts of energy persuading the black standouts to attend their schools.

One of the most productive hunting grounds for recruiters has been the city of Beaumont, Texas, where outstanding football players are almost commonplace, and where over the years there has grown up . . .

78

Billy Ray, the cab driver, turned off Washington Avenue, stopped his meter and slowly proceeded down a quiet, tree-sheltered street which was quickly giving way to darkness.

"Two hours ago," he said, "this place was crawling with kids."

He stopped near the entrance to the swimming pool and looked across the grassy park which was now hushed, motionless, abandoned in favor of last calls to supper and homework dealt by teachers uncaring of the fact that just one more series of downs might have meant a come-from-behind victory for one of the pick-up teams which calls Liberia Community Park its home field. "Man, I've seen some of the great ones out there. I mean *really* great ones — Bubba, Mel, Miller, Jerry, Jess ..."

We did not get out because Billy Ray is partially paralyzed from the waist down; the result of a summer game of "pass-touch" in this park which sits on the south side of Beaumont, Texas.

"Yeah, we called it 'pass-touch' but it got a little rougher than that. Just ask me, I'll tell ya. That's why I'm driving this cab 'stead of playing me some ball somewhere right now."

There is only token attempt at camouflaging the regret. Billy Ray is one of the Beaumont football players you have never heard of yet there was a time when he played and sweated and competed with some who are familiar to anyone with so much as a passing interest in the game. A spinal injury suffered one steamy Gulf Coast summer long ago has reduced him to a sideline observer, yet his eyes still burn with enthusiasm as he recalls those days when he still had "the moves."

"I saw Jerry (Levias) on the Johnny Carson Show one night," he says, "and when they asked him where he was from he said, 'Beaumont, Texas — Football Capital of the World.'

"No doubt about that; no doubt at all ..."

It's a shipping port/lumber mill city of 130,000, located an hour's drive west of Houston. You can't miss it: Just take highway 90 and stop before you get to the Louisiana state line. Three miles south of town is what remains of the famous Spindletop oil field, first major oil development in the United States.

And after a quick run through the rosters of the National Football League, one is hard pressed to argue Levias's claim that it is something of a monument to pro football. The city could, in all good conscience, list the output of pro talent as one of its major industries.

Residents can call them off from rote memory: Levias, Bubba Smith, Jesse Phillips, Mel Farr, Miller Farr, Warren Wells, Wayne Moore, Gus Hollomon, Lawrence 'Tody' Smith, Dwight Harrison, Charles Ford, Johnny Fuller, etc.

"Those," says Charles Levias, Jerry's father, "are just some of those playing right now. There are a bunch more who have retired or were cut after a short while or are playing up in the Canadian League. We had five boys drafted in 1971 alone."

With the exception of Hollomon and Fuller, the above mentioned players are all products of what is generally referred to as Beaumont's black community, an area cornerstoned by modest frame houses, friendly faces, and the square block of grass and trees known as Liberia Park.

"People are always asking me if I come from a ghetto," says the engaging little Levias. "I guess because I'm black and an athlete, a lot of people just seem to expect it, but, no, we lived in a pretty nice neighborhood. And the park made it even better."

There, youngsters of all ages spend their free hours engaging in endless games and foot races. A man like Bubba Smith or Jerry Levias is their Horatio Alger. At Liberia Community Park, much as it is on the campus of Grambling College, professional football is the Great American Dream.

80

That, then, is what makes Beaumont special: the park, the legends which surround it, and those who still come back to play in it.

Any football scout happening by in early July without benefit of its storied history might well rupture something getting to the nearest phone to report back to his boss at State U. that he had just struck the Mother Lode.

Consider if you will the roll call of those gathered in Beaumont during those weeks before they were to report to their respective camps prior to a recent pro season.

The Farr brothers were there, the Smiths were there, Phillips, Levias, Wells and Philadelphia linebacker Tony Guillory were there. So were Hollomon and Moore.

Denver running back Tom Smiley and Minnesota receiver Gene Washington had driven over from Port Arthur, twelve miles away. Clarence Williams, the Los Angeles cornerback who is a second cousin to the Farrs and Levias, was there. As were Kansas City defensive end Aaron Brown and Jets tackle Winston Hill. Chicago receiver Linzy Cole drove down from Dallas because Wells had promised to help him with his pass routes.

Over the years the word has spread throughout the NFL that the park in Beaumont is an ideal place for pre-training camp workouts, not to mention the fact that the food prepared by Mrs. Georgia Smith, coordinator of home economic teachers in the Beaumont Independent School District, seems literally to flow from the kitchen.

Another pro season behind him, her son Bubba sat, draped across the couch in the den of the fashionable Smith home, a gift pro football enabled him to give to his parents.

He, like others who look upon Liberia Park as something akin to a place of worship, refers to it simply as "the park."

"There was never a lot of horsing around out there back when I was in high school," he says. "It was always serious business. Still is.

"I guess I was in junior high when I first started go-

81

ing over there. It was right after we moved here. I'd tag along with Willie Ray (oldest of the three Smith sons) when he was in high school. We'd have all day track meets or throw the ball around and get up a game that went on and on until it got too dark to see.

"When I got to high school, we had practices twice a day during the summer months, one at six in the morning and another at four. That way, those who had jobs could work out before they went to work and again after they got off. If a guy didn't come out to the park in the summer it was just like saying he didn't want to play in the fall.

"We'd choose up sides and play," he recalls, "and the games never ended. We always just started off the next day where we had left off the day before."

On hand would always be a collection of athletes ranging from high school freshmen to the veteran professionals. When a player like Bubba Smith graduates from high school he does not bid farewell to the park. It simply becomes the site of workouts while preparing for preseason drills at Michigan State or Baltimore.

Jess Phillips, Cincinnati running back, grew up across the street from the Smith family and is quick to point out that "some of the most deadly serious games I've ever played took place in that park in Beaumont."

"A lot of times we would wind up punching each other. I mean, it was for blood. I remember having a big fight with Tody once and the guy lived right across the street. Man, his house was my house and mine was his — we were close — but we took those games pretty seriously."

He delights in recalling the summer Willie Ray brought home one of his University of Kansas teammates for the summer. "He brought this skinny-looking guy out to the park and it was a long time before we'd let him play because all the spots were filled. His name was Gale Sayers."

The last time anyone bothered to sit down and count them, Beaumont had sent more than two dozen players off to varying degrees of professional stardom. Though there is no official confirmation from Pete Rozelle's office, the local Chamber of Commerce claims the record and will challenge you to name any half-dozen Pennsylvania coal mines of your choosing which can come close.

The two individuals most responsible for this steady flow of talent are Willie Ray Smith, Sr., head coach at Charlton-Pollard High — and the only father I know who has had three sons sign professional contracts and seen two of them selected in the first round of the draft — and Clifton Ozen, head coach at Herbert High.

All-Negro schools until Texas integrated its school systems, they are but three miles removed from each other and boast a combined enrollment of less than 3,000. In the field house at Charlton-Pollard are pictures of seven former Bulldogs now playing in the pro ranks. The trophy case of the Herbert Panthers boasts a like number.

Smith, a wisp of a man who will enter his thirtieth year of high school coaching this fall, holds a slight edge over his friendly rival Ozen, thanks to the years he spent coaching at nearby Orange before moving to Beaumont in 1958. Among his players there were Ernie Ladd, former standout for Houston, Kansas City and San Diego, Garland Boyette, former Houston linebacker, and his brother, Claude, formerly with Denver.

Ozen is quick to point out that Smith gained unfair advantage by home growing three of his products. "You take those sons away," he grins, "and we've got a tie."

The two form an interesting contrast.

Smith, who never played a down of football because of a crippled leg, the result of a boyhood hunting accident, never really intended to be a coach. Ozen, an All-State tackle at the school where he now coaches, is doing what he's always wanted to do.

Smith, who has posted a remarkable record of 235

83

wins, 75 losses and 15 ties, teaches the wide open attack, the bomb, multiple offensive alignments; the brand of ball which rattles the scoreboard like a pinball machine. Ozen, who has a 110-28-4 record in his thirteen years as a head coach, is the conservative; the grind-it-out tactician who preaches fundamental truths like blocking and tackling.

"I graduated from Prarie View A&M with a degree in agriculture," Smith recalls, "and got a job teaching in Lufkin, Texas. It was wartime and there was nobody around to coach the football team so I got the job."

Much of his philosophy can be traced back to the noon recesses at Lufkin Dunbar High where he watched youngsters as they designed free-lance formations on the playground. "I'd see them work up a play, diagramming it in the dirt with a stick," he says, "and later that afternoon we'd work on it in practice."

Today he is a knowledgeable football man who is looked upon as an expert at judging talent by college coaches in search of material. When Michigan State's Duffy Daugherty came to town to sign Bubba, it was the elder Smith who suggested it might be well worth the Spartan coach's time to travel over to the tiny community of LaPorte and visit a young receiver named Gene Washington. After joining Bubba on the All-America teams while at Michigan State, Washington became a fixture with the Minnesota Vikings.

"Dad," says Bubba, "never gets excited but he has a way with kids. They'll play for him. He's the kind of coach who can tell you something without saying a word. He can just look at you and communicate. He's one helluva guy, I'll tell you that.

"A few years ago, Dad called me and Tody home to Beaumont after the season. Pollard had gone something like 7-3, Tody's Southern Cal team had been 6-4 and the Colts hadn't done worth a damn. We didn't even make it into the playoffs.

"My old man sat us down at the kitchen table and

84

said, 'We all had bad years — I mean bad — and we're not going to have another one.' That summer he nearly worked us to death. Run, run, run — every day. That next fall, Tody had a good year and was a No. 1 draft choice, Dad's team went undefeated, and we beat Dallas in the Super Bowl.

"The next time we sat down at the kitchen table he just sorta grinned, lit up a cigarette, and said, 'Now, that's more like it.' "

One might, with some good reason, guess that the 285-pound All-Pro young man passing out the bouquets would rank as the best player his father has ever coached. Not so. Neither is Ladd, nor Ladd's uncles, the Boyettes. Nor for that matter is it son Tody or neighbor Phillips.

That particular distinction is the property of his oldest son, Willie Ray, Jr., a six-foot, 190 pound running back whose horizons were lowered by knee surgery during his senior year at Kansas.

"He had it all," says the elder Smith. "Great moves, 9.5 speed, hands . . . everything you need to make it big. I've watched him score five touchdowns in a high school game more than once."

Despite the surgery which was performed midway through his senior year at KU, the Kansas City Chiefs drafted Willie Ray in the eleventh round, but a second operation became necessary the following fall. After a season with the Chiefs he was released and a comeback try with Buffalo a few years ago lasted only until holdout O. J. Simpson finally signed his contract.

Ozen ranks Wells, a youngster he had to persuade to come out for football, as the greatest he's coached, or for that matter, ever seen in high school ball.

"Miller Farr was easily the best running back and Mel was probably the most underrrated player and Jerry, well, I'd have to say he was the most amazing. Everything that boy has ever done has amazed me."

Levias, recalls Ozen, began his football association as a manager for the junior high team. "He was so little that he had a hard time carrying the water bucket."

In fact, Jerry, a victim of polio at age twelve, had been told by his parents that he was too small to be playing football and thus had to solicit the help of his sister, Charlena, to sneak off to practice.

"She was pretty good at finding ways for me to get out of the house so I could go over to the park during the summer. In the fall, I told my parents I had signed up as manager again," the San Diego receiver recalls.

It wasn't until the 116-pound freshman defensive back who had told the coaches his name was "Levniaz" was delivered at the doorstep unconscious following a workout injury that the Levias family learned it had a football player and not a manager in the house.

After that, Charles Levias decided to permit his son to play, as long as his grades remained at a high level.

A Beaumont lumber yard employee, Mr. Levias began to realize that athletics might well enable his son to become the first college-educated Levias.

"I didn't ever want him to have a pick and shovel in his hand," he says. "I wanted him to be able to develop a talent and use it to make himself a good living. Football helped Jerry to do that and I'm proud of him."

Doubtless, that same story could be told in a number of Beaumont homes.

Ozen delights in recalling some of the backfields he has had at Charlton-Pollard.

Like the year he had Mel Farr at quarterback and Levias and Don Bean at halfbacks. "Mel could run the hundred in about ten-flat which is pretty good for a quarterback, but boy, he sure looked slow with Jerry and Don (both 9.7 sprinters) back there."

And while those who have worn the colors of Pollard and Herbert are legends in their own rights, the annual battle between the two schools ranks as one of autumn's primary conversation pieces.

Somewhere along the way it was labeled "the Soul Bowl" and the name has stuck. "The name fits," grins

Ozen, "because, believe me, there's a lot of soul there when our kids get together to play. It gets kinda wild."

Because it is sure to draw an overflow crowd of 20,000 or more it is played in the larger Lamar Tech University stadium rather than the public schools stadium and it is said that if you aren't there by five o'clock in the afternoon you won't be among those sitting in the stands for the 8 p.m. kickoff.

The late September battle is almost always for the District 21-AAAA championship and is living, breathing proof of that standard notion that "you can throw out the record books when . . . " Ticket scalpers have a field day and a good part of a week's earnings is often wagered on one's alma mater. College scouts fly in like so many vultures and football fans from surrounding communities like Silsbee and Jasper and Kirbyville drive up for the game.

Levias likens it to a carnival. "It's fun," he says, "but people take the outcome seriously. Like, if you were going with a girl and she went to the other school, you didn't talk to her the week of the game. Herbert guys who had grown up and married Pollard girls would split up once they got inside the gates and each would go to his or her school's side."

Bubba Smith recalls his final game against Herbert High with obvious fondness. It didn't demand the national attention of his appearance against Notre Dame when he and his Michigan State teammates battled the Irish to a 10-10 tie in the 1966 version of the Game of the Decade. Nor was it worth the kind of payoff the Colts' Super Bowl victory over Dallas earned him, yet there is a revered place for the 24-20 victory he and his Pollard teammates won.

"Mel and I had this thing going about trying to outdo each other," he recalls. "It dated back to our junior high days.

"We palled around together a lot, going over to girls' houses, that sort of thing, but when we got on the foot-

87

ball field we really got after it against each other."

In what was to be their final schoolboy battle, Farr was cast in the role of quarterback and linebacker for Herbert and Smith was a center and middle guard for Pollard.

"Both teams were undefeated going into the game," Bubba points out, "and our guys were thinking we were pretty hot stuff. We had our shoes all taped up and that sort of thing. You know, flashy high school stuff.

"Well, Mel was hot as a firecracker and I wasn't getting to him much and they had a 20-6 halftime lead. Dad came in the dressing room and told us to get all that damn tape and junk off our shoes and get ready to play ball the second half or we were going to be riding home in a pretty quiet bus. Then he just walked out of the room."

From that point Coach Smith takes the story: "I'm still not sure what all went on in that dressing room but they came out and really got after it in the second half. Bubba was all over Mel, constantly dropping him for big losses."

Bubba grins. "We finally took the lead in the game and with just a few seconds left on the clock we had the ball. We didn't even call a play. I would just snap the ball to the quarterback and he would fall on it and that would be it.

"Man, I was so tired I didn't even lift my head after snapping the ball."

If he had, he would have seen linebacker Farr crashing toward him to deliver a knee to the side of his head.

"He knocked me out cold," Bubba remembers. "That's how intense the rivalry was. After the game he apologized and we went to a party together."

Football in Beaumont, Texas, then, is many things: recreation, recognition, fierce competition, a means to an end, an obsession, the brass ring youngsters try to catch. The game here is something special. Perhaps more so than in other similar football hotbeds across the United States.

Why?

"The kids here, especially the Negroes, have a very limited recreational outlet," explains Willie Ray Smith. "Therefore, we encourage them to stay in the park and play.

"Kids have seen how successful some of our former players have gone on to become and they make up their minds that they want a shot at the same kind of thing.

"For many years, a Negro going to college could get a degree and become a school teacher and that was about it. Oh, there would be a few go into the medical profession and maybe a lawyer or two, or a dentist, but you could count those on one hand. It's better now but it's still a long haul.

"Pro football is what the Negro calls 'instant rich' and the prospects provide a strong incentive. Take Bubba, for instance: The money he made in two, three hours in the Super Bowl would take me three years to earn."

At Herbert High, Ozen's budget provides for twenty-five new footballs each fall before practices begin. There are never any left over from the previous year.

Some evening, just as summer is beginning, he loads all the old balls into his car and drives through the black community, leaving them in yards selected at random or in a barrow ditch here and there. Sometimes he spirals a few into the park.

Thus one seldom sees a youngster in south Beaumont who does not have a football.

"As soon as the kids begin to show an interest in football," he says, "they set imaginary goals to be like Mel or Jerry or Bubba.

"We repeatedly remind them of those who have made it big and whenever a former player is in town, he comes by and talks with the kids. Our good athletes go into college with a pro contract in mind.

"The desire to become a professional football player is more than an ambition here. It's more like a tradition."

Smith and Ozen are both quick to deny that they

have cornered the market. When Chicago picked University of Houston defensive back Charles Ford in the '71 draft he became the first Beaumont High graduate ever selected by the pros. The Jets' Hollomon attended French High and San Francisco cornerback Johnny Fuller is a graduate of South Park. Forest Park saw its first player drafted in 1969 when the Jets picked Cliff Larson. Denver selected South Park's Dwight Harrison in the second round in '71.

And in the summers they'll all be over at Liberia Park, bringing friends and teammates with them, cultivating the legend that Beaumont is the nation's leading producer of football talent.

There, young boys will join them, minus the supervision of coaches, dreaming their special dreams and mimicking the floating, rhythmic style of a pro receiver or trudging through windsprints in the same head-bobbing gait of their favorite pro cornerback. In the park, every day is Sunday afternoon.

Here, they never stop honoring their heroes. It's not hard to get someone to recall for you the time Bubba Smith held David "Big Daddy" Lattin, the pro basketball star, to just two points in a Negro high school all-star game. Or how Tody Smith and a group of Texas high school graduates went up to Pennsylvania one summer and defeated a team of football all-stars from that state. Or how Miller Farr was a good enough shortstop as a schoolboy to receive a bonus offer from the Pittsburgh Pirates.

"You know," Ozen points out, "there's a school out in Oakland, California, McClymonds High School, which has come close to the tradition we have here. It has produced basketball player Bill Russell, Olympic sprint champion Jim Hines and baseball greats like Curt Flood, Vade Pinson and Frank Robinson. Man, that's pretty fast company."

"Yeah," Smith agrees, "but you have to remember, Frank Robinson was actually born here in Beaumont."

"The essence of the game is transformation. In the medieval pageant peasants became angels and commoners kings. In more familiar settings sixteen-year-old boys in white T-shirts and blue jeans are transformed under their golden helmets into transitory deities, bearers of a town's pride and saviors of its waylaid passions. . . . "

— *from Saturday Review*

HEROES IN THE HINTERLAND

There is very little to say about this next piece except that it ranks as one of my personal favorites. While I cannot guess how it would be judged by those on the lookout for all the mechanical elements that are supposed to be included in prize-winning journalism, I do know that I felt a rare kind of satisfaction, a feeling that I had said what I wanted to say, when it was finally pulled from the typewriter.

At the time it was written, it was my happy fate to be residing on a small farm/ranch whose main gate was, as the crow flies, nine miles removed from even a loaf of bread. While the location created some problems when the stabbing urge for a pizza developed just as the Late, Late Show was coming on, there were no next door neighbors to break the creative thoughts by asking for the loan of a cup of sugar or a shoulder to cry on.

Until that time when the proud owner passed on to

his Great Reward, leaving his 350 acres to heirs who had other plans for the place, I learned something of the luxury of bucolic living, often going for long stretches of time in which I would venture no farther away than the mailbox which was strategically located a mile away on Farm-to-Market 2005. It was, in all respects, the ideal place for a Bearded Dreamer.

When words would not make the proper transition from brain to typewriter, there was a simple cure; take fishing pole in hand, walk south 200 yards, and sit on the bank of a small lake populated by perch, an occasional catfish and more turtles than you could shake a stick at. While it may never be my station in life to rise to any great stature in the world of letters, I doubt that there are many of your Literary Giants out there today who have between rough draft and final manuscript, known the excitement of watching a covey of quail feed in the front yard. Or, in a hike from back door to back fence, seen wild turkey, a fox, rabbits, a family of armadillos, two hyperactive bee trees, one rattlesnake and various other products of the out-of-doors.

I gained such handy knowledge as how to eliminate a hive of bees from a chimney, how to chop firewood without turning city boy hands into masses of blisters, how to prevent the backing up of a septic tank in times of plentiful rain and how to prime the pump in times when there was no rain at all. I also feel I learned something relative to my chosen craft.

He who would insist that there is not a degree of loneliness attached to this business of storytelling has never boarded himself into a room with only a typewriter, a stack of blank white paper and his private thoughts for companionship.

There were, in fact, times when the peace and quiet became so peaceful and quiet that I would gladly have blown up the church of my choice simply for the pleasure of hearing the boom.

Thus it was that there came times when it became

necessary in the name of sanity to take leave of the solitary contentment and satisfy myself that there were still people out there who did things other than send notes down from some Manhattan skyscraper advising me of the status of my latest literary offering.

It was with no small degree of excitement, then, that I learned one early September that a community but a few miles up the road listed among its buildings a high school. The Star Tigers, playing a game known as six-man football, went to battle under the lights each Thursday night in one of the purest atmospheres of amateur sport I have ever witnessed.

With no urging I came to look forward to those evenings when after a hurried supper I would drive over and pay the fifty cents admission fee for a 50-yard-line seat from which to watch my . . .

Heroes In The Hinterland

Star, Texas, is one of those chicken-in-the-front-yard hamlets which provides nearby farmers and ranchers a place to get gas, buy groceries, attend church, mail a letter or meet to see whose rain gauge registered most during a previous evening's thunderstorm. It sits at the junction of Highway 84 and Farm-to-Market 1047, quiet, peaceful and claiming a population of 107 people.

On the southernmost edge of town, past empty remnants of a drug store, lumber yard and bus stop, stands Star School, a sandstone monument to the WPA program. Inside one will find classrooms filled with wood and wrought iron desks from another time in academic history, ten teachers, 88 students making up grades 1-12 (there are 34 students in high school) and the same ebullient, youthful enthusiasm that is characteristic of public schools regardless of the size of the student body.

Having successfully managed to stay a step ahead of the Texas Education Agency's consolidation program, the Star public school draws students from a widespread school district with a population of 350.

93

And barring some disaster of nature most of those will be on hand when Coach Grant Tidwell's Star Tigers kick off against whatever District 7-B rival the schedule has to offer.

For the 38-year-old Tidwell, breakfast is a chore on Thursdays. Not so much because it is eaten in the pre-dawn gray which precedes sun-up but rather because it launches what football coaches, players and fans universally refer to as Game Day.

Though he has gone through seven years of Game Days as coach at Star High it is always the same: he is tense, bursting with nervous energy and smokes more than usual — though never in front of his players. A winner of three consecutive district championships, Grant Tidwell still is a name you have likely not heard before.

While he practices his chosen craft in a state which ofttimes reveres high school football coaches over poets and scientists and pays them better to prove it, Tidwell and fifty-nine other Texas coaches whose youngsters participate in the free-wheeling, high-scoring, wide-open game known as six-man football are celebrities only to the 150-200 who turn out for their games each week.

Tidwell's finest hour, a 72-36 victory over the Carbon Wolverines in the 1971 Region II championship game, capping an 11 wins-1 loss season, hardly sent the reporters who man the state wire services dashing to the nearest typewriter. When tiny Marathon saw its six-man victory streak snapped after forty consecutive wins, the reaction of sportswriter across the state was less than consoling. "Where in the hell is Marathon?" one asked.

It is a game reserved for schools with an enrollment of 100 students or less, the battlegrounds are dot-on-the-map communities which would try the geographic knowledge of life-long Texans — Cherokee, Gustine and Sidney; Mullin, Pottsville and May — and the adversaries are teams of Indians, Bulldogs, and Bobcats drilled by one-man coaching staffs and played on fields poorly lighted and lined with automobiles filled with people who view

94

their weekly war games through windows freshly cleaned at Lee's Grocery and Gulf Station.

"If a man is after publicity and recognition as the world's greatest coach," Tidwell understates, "six-man football is the wrong place for him to be."

An athlete of modest achievement for the Class B Blanket High Tigers, a team which managed to play eleven-man football by the slimmest of enrollment margins, he had neither encouragement nor the talent to continue playing while attending Howard Payne College. Instead, he concentrated his efforts toward a degree in social studies with a minor in physical education.

"I knew even in high school that the only way I could stay around athletics would be either as a fan sitting in the stands, yelling my head off, or as a coach. I felt I could make more of a contribution as a coach."

After three years as a junior high coach at Pearland, Texas, he applied for the job at Star. Its duties, as outlined by superintendent Leroy Beard, were to teach classes in world history, American government, civics, girls' physical education, coach all the school's athletic teams, junior high and high school, and drive a school bus.

"I had never even seen a six-man football game," Tidwell recalls, "but I told the superintendent that I would like to take the job for a couple of years, then try for an assistant coach position at a larger school."

That was seven years and several job offers ago.

"It's simple," he says. "I like it here. There is a place in our society for the rural school. I'm happy with what I'm doing and feel that our athletic program is as important to our students as those operated by larger schools."

The enthusiasm of the community lends credence to his observation. While the late evening chores demanded of farm and ranch life prevent the organization of an official booster club like those found in most towns, Tidwell is one of those few coaches in the state who has players' parents willing to travel to other towns to scout future opponents, returning with such data as forma-

95

tions, weights, heights and grade classification of rival team members.

"I try," Tidwell explains, "to ask only the fathers of boys playing on the junior high team (which plays its game on Tuesday nights) so no one will have to miss watching his own son play on Thursday."

While school board members in Philadelphia recently questioned the worth of athletics in its 38 public schools and Los Angeles dropped junior-high football in the name of sounder economics, Star maintains both a junior-high team (19 youngsters from grades 5-8) and a high school team (11 boys, grades 9-12) with an operational budget of less than $2,000 a year, a figure which would not buy equipment for many of the state's Class AAAAA schools.

"Yes," admits superintendent Beard, "athletics puts a financial strain on us at times but we feel it is a very worthwhile investment."

By necessity, six-man schools like Star learn to cut corners in areas many schools would never consider. While larger schools film all of their games (and sometimes even practice sessions), Tidwell feels fortunate if he is able to film a couple of games a season. Players purchase their own meals on out-of-town trips and members of the junior high team must provide their own football shoes. "I like for them to wear cleats," Tidwell says, "but if they can't afford them, it's okay with me if they play in tennis shoes or bare-footed."

Equipment is more often repaired than replaced. "I think I've bought four new sets of shoulder pads in the past six years," he says. "One of our teachers has a friend who coaches at Southwest Texas State and a few years ago he gave us quite a bit of equipment that they no longer needed. We've put it to good use."

Rural school teacher-coaches, depending on their longevity, will earn salaries in the $6,500-8,000 range, considerably below the $12,000-$17,500 earned by some coaches laboring at larger schools.

96

In addition to coaching the junior high (from 1:30 to 2:30 p.m.) and the high school (2:30 to 3:30) football teams, Tidwell coaches junior high (boys and girls) basketball in the winter and track in the spring.

Of the estimated 10 million fans who turn out to see high school football in Texas each fall, only a small percentage of them have seen or are even aware of six-man games. If they know the game, they are aware that there are a number of rules which differ from those applied on fields where 11-man teams play.

The game is played on a field 80 yards long rather than the customary 100; six-man teams must travel 15 yards for a first down rather than ten, a kicked conversion is worth two points and one if made by running or passing (just opposite of the 11-man rule); and a successful field goal earns a team four points rather than the generally recognized three. Six-man teams play ten minute quarters rather than the twelve used in 11-man schoolboy games and all players, the center included, are eligible to receive passes.

It is a game played by youngsters who entertain little hope of ever attracting the attention of college scouts willing to offer them books, tuition and fees to continue their athletics at some major university.

"In the seven years I've been here," Tidwell says with no attempt to mask his disdain, "there has been one college coach come by to see if we had any prospects — a TCU assistant back in 1968.

"I've had several players who might have made it at a small college if someone had just given them the opportunity. That, I guess, is one of my personal goals — to see one of my players get a college scholarship."

Tidwell's frustration — the refusal of men who coach 11-man teams to accept the six-man game as something more than pass-touch in pads — can be traced back to the very birth of the game.

Six-man football began in 1934, the brainchild of a Chester, Nebraska educator-coach named Stephen Epler who recognized a void in the fall activities of smaller schools. Searching for a solution, he went to the drawing board and designed a football game which would not require the customary 11 players.

As word of his new athletic concept spread so did interest in the game. States throughout the Midwest adopted Epler's plan and in 1938, Rodney Kidd, then athletic director of the Texas Interscholastic League, governing body of the state's schoolboy sport, wrote Epler for information on the game.

"We contacted a couple of coaches at small schools, Prairie Lea and Martindale, in the spring and asked them if they would study the rules, practice for a while, and put on an exhibition game for us so that we might see what the game was all about."

They liked what they saw and the following fall such previously non-football playing schools as Dripping Springs, Harrold and Oklaunion and the two squads which had staged the exhibition were sporting their first district championships.

The game's popularity reached a national peak in 1953, when 30,000 teams across the country participated in six-man football. Today, however, the consolidation of rural schools nationwide has turned the game into nothing more than a scrapbook memory for most states. The remaining outposts of the game are to be found in Texas and Missouri, where a few schools still compete on the six-man level, New York, where it is part of the intramural program, and in Saskatchewan, Canada, where half the province's 90 high schools play six-man ball.

In Texas, the UIL recognized an all-time high of 48 six-man districts in 1941 and today counts 60 teams playing in twelve districts located primarily in West and Central sections of the state. Still enthusiasm for the game is such that an annual East-West All Star game is conducted in late summer and plans were eventually approved for a state championship series modeled after the 11-man playoffs.

And though the list of Texas' six-man graduates who have made names for themselves on a higher athletic plane is admittedly thin there have been exceptions.

Cristoval's Jack Pardee earned nationwide recognition as a Texas A&M fullback in the '50s and is now in his seventeenth year of professional football as a member of the Washington Redskins. Gene Mayfield, head coach at West Texas State University, got his football initiation quarterbacking the six-man Quitaque Panthers, and Emory Bellard, head coach at Texas A&M, earned his first letter as a sophomore member of the Port Aransas High team.

"There is a myth," says Star principal Earl Jones, "that the rural school doesn't adequately prepare a youngster for college. This is an excuse you'll hear from some college coaches for not considering six-man players."

"All they have to do is check our record. Last year we graduated nine seniors and all are in college and doing quite well."

Tidwell points to former players like Bert Geeslin who was voted the top science student at Baylor last year and Earl Hall who is now working on his Masters at Sam Houston state. Gary Boykin is in his third year at North Texas State, raising a family, making good grades, and Charles Miles is in his sophomore year at Tidwell's alma mater, Howard Payne.

To the man, the last time they had on a football uniform was when they posed for the post-season team picture in their senior year at Star High School.

It was 7 a.m. and Tidwell was behind the wheel of a yellow school bus, grinding down a country road en route to pick up the first of the 21 youngsters on his 16-mile route.

"You know," he said, making conversation through the rear view mirror, "I'm not really sure I would know how to handle some of the discipline problems I hear

99

about other coaches having. The simple truth is that I've just never had to deal with anything like that here.

"Take the kids we have on the team this year, for instance; ten of them work on the farm or ranch every day when they get home from practice. The other boy helps his dad run the service station over at Center City, and hauls hay. Football isn't all that hard for them — it's an escape from work for an hour or so. It's fun and it means something to them."

Shortly after eight the bus arrives at school and Tidwell prepares for a morning of teaching. After one afternoon class he changes into a sweat suit and reports to the football field to put the junior high team through its paces, then lines the field, checks to see that every one's game uniform is in his locker, and telephones the game officials to make sure they will be there. "That's why we play our games on Thursdays," he explains. "We can get better officials. You won't get the good ones on Fridays when the bigger schools can pay them more." (Payment of officials is determined by the attendance, thus working a six-man game will rarely earn any of the three men who call the game more than the $10 minimum.)

Since there is no 2:30 practice for the high school team on the day of a game the players huddle in the cramped, almost airless dressing room for skull practice before the student body gathers for a pep rally.

"I can't tell you what kind of team we'll have this year," Tidwell tells an enthusiastic student body between the yells led by six cheerleaders, "but I can tell you this: we've got the kind of players who will give everything they've got. I think you'll be proud of them tonight . . . " A flood of cheers drown his final words.

At 3:30 he re-traces his bus route, returning the students home, promising along the way to see them later at the game. "Beat Oglesby," one girl says as she steps off the bus.

At five o'clock Tidwell is home with only time to clean up, change into his good-luck red shirt and drink a

100

glass of iced tea before beginning his trip back to school. He stops at the grocery store for a bag of ice which will be applied to the sprains and bruises his players are likely to suffer during the course of the game.

As the countdown begins for the 8 p.m. kick-off he tapes his players' ankles, goes to an adjacent dressing room to welcome the visiting coach and talks briefly with the game officials.

"Good men," Tidwell says. "I've had them before. No problems there."

An hour later the Star cheerleaders and the 19-girl pep squad (the school has no band), all dressed in school colors of red and black, are well into the yell routines and two girls representing the Junior Class are making their way through the crowd selling two-for-a-quarter chances on a cake they had baked in home-making class. By the time the lucky number is drawn at halftime they will have earned eight dollars which will go into a fund for the end of the year athletic banquet.

On the sidelines, Tidwell is almost passive, a marked contrast to the rival coach across the way who constantly paces, yelling instructions to his players. The public address announcer mentions for maybe the tenth time that "a key to a Ford automobile has been found and can be claimed here at the announcer's booth." He later announces with considerable embarrassment that the lost key fits the ignition of his own car.

Late in the first quarter senior tailback Marvin Hunt breaks on an 87-yard touchdown run which sets the Tigers off and running toward a 34-20 victory. Throughout the game Tidwell methodically goes about his duties, sending in plays, giving a quick rubdown to a player who has limped off the field with a leg cramp and nodding approvingly to players who have carried out their assignments well.

Long before the game was over it was obvious that his players had things well under control.

He accepted congratulatory handshakes from de-

101

lighted fans as the game ended, waved in acknowledgement to the honking car horns and trotted toward the dressing room. There he talked quietly to his victorious players, conservative in his praise, pointing out that there was still a long season ahead. He waited until everyone had showered, dressed and left, then turned out the lights, locked the gym door and returned to the field to pull the switch that turned the stadium to darkness.

Upon arriving home he placed a long distance call to the Abilene paper, giving a brief rundown of the victory, then settled himself at the dining room table to record the statistics a manager had kept during the game.

By midnight he had eaten a sandwich his wife had prepared, washed it down with a glass of milk, and was relaxed, ready for bed.

Game Day, all 18 hours of it, had been both satisfying and successful.

7

"What Jim Norman did when he came here was get everyone so busy they no longer had time to worry about the color of the other guy's skin. Because of him, the whole community — not just the football team — became a winner.

— a big Sandy football fan

BIG TIME IN BIG SANDY

There is a cliche attached to high school football which suggests that with the proper degree of success, the coach of the local team enjoys enough popularity to be elected mayor of the town. Such was the case with Jim Norman, a man who turned a quiet little community which had long taken it's Friday night victories whenever they came into a pluperfect powerhouse.

But, he modestly points out, he could not have served as efficiently as mayor had he not had a hard-working city manager lending an able hand. And his football program might not have been quite as successful had it not been for a gifted running back named David Overstreet who went on to college and professional stardom.

Combining efforts, however, then turned the autumn months into a . . .

Big Time In Big Sandy

For Jim Norman it is a normal Friday afternoon in September. In his tiny field house office which is clut-

103

tered with various pieces of football hardware and too many people, he is trying with remarkable success to accomplish several chores at once.

As head football coach for the Big Sandy High School Fighting Wildcats, Norman is running down a checklist of last-minute details which need his attention in the few hours remaining before his team's first home game of the season. And as mayor of the quiet little East Texas community of 1,022 residents, he is holding court with his city manager, who has arrived with payroll checks Norman must sign for Big Sandy's half-dozen city employees and bids received on a new typewriter for the city secretary.

On game days Norman's hectic schedule at the school where he is social studies teacher, assistant principal and coach makes it impossible for him to get downtown to city hall. Instead, city politics come to the field house, hand delivered by city manager Skippy McWilliams.

Norman quickly signs the checks, then attends to the bids. "This one looks reasonable to me," he says. "Let's go with it." McWilliams simply nods in agreement. It is unlikely that he would argue with the decision any more than Wildcat quarterback Stan Shipp will dispute Norman's play selections during tonight's game. The municipal matter settled, Norman turns his attention to the towel-clad offensive tackle who is standing in the doorway leading to the dressing room, asking how to adjust the temperature on the whirlpool bath. "Get the manager to set it at 110 degrees," Norman says, "and keep that sore leg in it for 10 minutes — no longer. Then get out and dress. Pep rally's at 3:30."

As the youngster takes leave, Norman turns in his swivel chair and addresses the group in his office adjoining the athletic dressing room. "Now there's an example of a kid who just needs a little special attention. He was failing math, just not doing the work, and his teacher came to me. I told him to have the kid come in every afternoon with his assignment and I'd work with him.

Every day I sit him down over there at that table and go over the instructions with him and work one example problem. He takes it from there. The trouble was, it turns out, that he just couldn't understand the instructions. Now he's carrying an 86 average in math and working hard at it. He just needed a little extra help."

Then Norman quickly qualifies his statement, pointing out that no member of his football team is allowed to play unless he maintains passing grades. Teachers, he says, have offered in recent years to assign special papers designed to lift an athlete's failing grade to a passing standard so that he might be eligible to play. Without exception, Norman has refused the special favors. His players, he is fond of saying, earn the privilege of being a part of the Wildcats team by proving themselves first as students.

His discussion of scholarship is interrupted no less than a half-dozen times by the ring of the phone. A steady stream of diehard Big Sandy fans, unable to stay away from the field until time for the kickoff against New Diana, wander in and out. One informs Norman that he has just heard on the radio that the Wildcats had moved up to No. 2 in the Class A state rankings by virtue of their season opening win against Ore City. Another stopped by to wish the coach well before going over to the superintendent's office to pick up his season tickets. Yet another observes that the Wildcat's margin of victory will be determined by how often David Overstreet, the team's gifted halfback, carries the ball.

Somehow Norman manages to stay relaxed in the turbulent atmosphere. It is something he's been doing since he arrived six years ago in this sheltered part of the world where residents busy themselves with dairying, farming, pulpwood cutting, church activities, and glorying in the fortunes of the Big Sandy football team he coaches.

And indeed, the glories have been plentiful in recent years. As the Wildcats prepare to face New Diana, they have not been defeated in 42 straight games. They have won or shared the state championship for the last three years, while in Class B competition. Since Norman assumed the job as head coach the Wildcats have won 68, lost six and tied one. It is worthy of note that five of those six losses came in 1970, his first year on the job. Since that time only a 7-6 loss to New Waverly on December 5, 1972, has gone on the negative side of the Wildcat's won-lost ledger.

It has, however, not always been so. In fact, one has to go back to 1935 to find even so much as a district championship claimed by Big Sandy prior to Norman's arrival. Thus it is that big Sandy's football history prior to 1970 is ofttimes referred to as Before Jim Norman . . .

A native of Hernando, Mississippi, the 41-year-old Norman had decided in the spring of 1969 that he was going to get out of coaching and concentrate his efforts toward achieving an administrative position in some high school. Since his 1961 graduation from Delta State College, his coaching career had wound from Horn Lake, Mississippi, to Killeen, Texas, to Grapevine, where he worked four years as an assistant. He had resigned himself to the belief that a head coaching job was not part of his immediate future.

Then came a call from Big Sandy High superintendent Charles Penney. A small school with no winning tradition, less than ideal athletic facilities and simmering racial problems, it was looking for a man who could re-direct the program. Of the three men interviewed, Jim Norman was the man Penney and the school board felt could best handle the situation. That summer, Norman and his family moved to Big Sandy.

What he found was a sharply divided student body. "The blacks," he recalls, "didn't want to have anything to do with the whites, and the whites went out of their way to ignore the blacks. There was no violence, but I felt it was coming. What existed was a great indifference."

106

Racial unrest and Jim Norman were no strangers. "In the fall of 1962," he remembers, "I was going to begin my first year as a head coach at Horn Lake. That was the same year James Meredith decided to become the first black student at Ole Miss. So the week before our first game the National Guard unit of which I was a member was activated. My principal stood in for me as coach of our first game, and we lost 7-6. The second week I missed all the workouts and flew home from Oxford on Friday so I could coach the team. We lost that one 7-6, too.

Norman wasted no time in settling the problems in Big Sandy. He called a meeting in the school gym and heard the athletes out. Then, in a firm voice which would become familiar as days wore on, he said, "So far as I'm concerned boys are boys. I don't care what color you are, what church you go to, who your mommas and dads are. You boys are going to be my football team, and on my team everybody plays together."

Seventeen players reported for practice in the fall of 1970, a roster roughly a third the number which now annually checks out uniforms.

"What Coach Norman did," says Superintendent Penney, whose son is now a junior end for the Wildcats, "was get everybody so busy they didn't have time to worry about the color of the other guy's skin. If they weren't practicing or in meetings, they were out raising money to buy new equipment. The enthusiasm and dedication of the football players soon began spreading throughout the school — and into the community."

By the time Big Sandy captured its first state championship almost everyone in town was involved in some manner. Penney hand-painted yard markers for the football field. Dale Willis, the ag teacher, volunteered to film the Wildcats games so the team might have them for study. Principal Odis Hammock began driving the team bus to out-of-town games. Membership of the Quarterback Club rose to 100, a new high.

When Norman made the booster organization aware

that he was in need of new shoulder pads, a turkey shoot was immediately planned to raise the necessary funds. A pancake supper made it possible to buy an exercise machine for the field house. Norman, as the saying goes, became a popular enough figure in town to be elected mayor, should he choose to run. Which is exactly what happened after he and his Wildcats returned to Big Sandy with their second state championship in 1974.

Cyril Bennett is proud of the fact that he captained the first Big Sandy High School team ever fielded. That was in 1929. The 63-year-old Justice of the Peace also organized the first Quarterback Club, has served on the school board for the past 15 years and, save for a gall bladder operation which kept him bedridden for two miserable weeks a few years back, hasn't missed a Big Sandy football game since returning from service in Gen. George Patton's Third Army.

He is also the football program's chief fund raiser the one who assumes responsibility for chartering buses to out-of-town play-off games and is an unblushing advocate of Norman's philosophies.

"He moved in here," the Judge says flatly, "and saved this little town. He pulled it together, got everyone's thinking straightened out, and turned us into a winner. He'd be embarrassed to hear me say this, but he reminds me a little of Patton in that they both go into whatever it is they're doing to win."

It was Judge Bennett who first suggested that anyone who could run a football team well enough to win state championships might also be a good man to run the community. As election time approached, Jim Norman became his candidate for mayor.

"A group of us finally went to him and asked if he would run," Bennett says. "We explained that we weren't backing him simply because he had been a good football coach. He knew the problems of the community, and we felt he could do something about them."

Norman pondered the suggestion, discussed it with his wife Mary Lee and his four oldest children (Jimmy, 19, graduated from Big Sandy last year; Ricky, 17, is a senior guard on his dad's team; David, 15, is a sophomore quarterback; Margie, 14, is a freshman member of the BSHS band; and Trey, 4, is already showing pretty good moves and a strong arm), and tossed his hat into the political arena. He became the town's new mayor by margin of almost 50 votes.

Thus Norman's working days, already fragmented into responsibilities as teacher, coach, assistant principal, sponsor of the student council and senior class and active member of the First Baptist Church, were stretched even farther. His routine finds him checking in at city hall each morning before school, during the lunch hours and following afternoon football practices. On the first Tuesday of each month he presides over the monthly city council meeting. Spare time is not something Jim Norman has to excess.

"He's done a good job as mayor," says James Crow, who operates the Texaco station. "He's worked at it, just like he works at making that football team a winner. He's got us some better equipment for the fire department and improved the garbage collections and is getting some things done about the bad streets in town."

With six months of his term remaining, Norman insists he will not run for re-election. "It's really a bigger job than I had anticipated," he says, "one that requires a great deal more time than I've been able to give it. Naturally, my first priority is my job at the school, so there have been times when I've had to put my responsibilities as mayor aside. We've got a number of qualified people around town who can take over and do a good job. And there is a lot of work to be done."

In, for instance, the black neighborhood where approximately 30 percent of Big Sandy's population resides.

Townspeople refer to it simply as "over there." In

109

the weary tradition of the South, it is located across the railroad tracks, isolated from the other residential areas of town. The dreary rows of houses almost without exception are old, in crying need of paint and repairs and woefully overcrowded. There are no curbs along the streets. Wrecked shells of automobiles sit grotesquely in front yards. Clearly, it is a part of the world Urban Renewal and Big Sandy tax money have overlooked.

The building which once housed Excelsior Junior High now stands empty. Negro children used to attend it through eight grades before transferring to a black high school five miles up the road, closed in 1965 when integration opened the doors of Big Sandy High School to blacks. Linzy Bowie, former Excelsior principal, now holds the same job at the integrated elementary school and mans the ticket booth at football games. His red brick home is one of the nicest in the black community.

At midafternoon, Mrs. Murtis Overstreet leaves the laundromat. She is wearing slacks, house slippers and a yellow football jersey with the number 20 stitched on the back. It is the number her son David Overstreet, a young halfback who is the best player on the Wildcats team — best in the state, some say — will wear later this evening.

Mrs. Overstreet is in a hurry to complete her chores so that she can get to the stadium well before kickoff. Still, she takes time to talk of her five living children and the daughter who died at age 6 after a lifelong struggle with epilepsy and brain damage. Of the husband she has not seen since "sometime around 1968" and of being on welfare and of the series of nervous breakdowns she suffered after losing her daughter. When the talk turns to her 18-year-old son, her eyes light. David Overstreet, B-plus student, captain of the football team, a young athlete who will soon have the opportunity to take his pick of the major colleges in the United States, stands as living proof of her parental accomplishments. Life has not been easy for Murtis Overstreet, but Number 20 for the Big Sandy Wildcats has made her many worries more bearable.

At home, meanwhile, David Overstreet's only worry is a sore ankle he turned in the season opener when he rushed for 248 yards and scored three touchdowns. Sitting in the living room, awaiting a ride to the stadium with friends, he has read a letter from Frank Kush, head football coach at Arizona State, wishing him luck this season and reminding him of ASU's abiding interest in his academic and athletic future. David has been receiving such letters from a variety of colleges for the past year.

Setting the letter aside, he rubs the slightly sore ankle and talks in a modest, articulate fashion. "I'm gonna have to tape it tonight so I can cut. I think it'll be okay. My main goal right now is to do whatever I can to help us win another state championship. That's what I want most of all. What's good for the team is good for me. Then, if some honors come my way, that's extra. I'll be glad to have them, don't get me wrong, but the team comes first. We work together; that's why we win. And we've got a great coach. Coach Norman, he's a great man. He's treated us all good. Lotta times I've gone to him to talk about my problems. He always listens and wants to know what he can do to help."

Teamwork and outstanding coaching aside, there are few who will argue that without 6-foot-2, 194-pound David Overstreet, the Wildcats would be just another pretty good football team among the 1,000 public schools playing in Texas. From the time he quarterbacked the eighth grade team as a mere sixth grader, it has been obvious to all close followers of Big Sandy athletics that he was something special.

His statistics bear out their conviction. In his first three seasons, David rushed for 5,487 yards and 78 touchdowns. He scored 56 of those touchdowns in his junior year, missing the state scoring record by only one.

111

He was named to the All-State team and selected by the Amarillo Chamber of Commerce as the Texas High School Football Player of the Year.

Football coaches throughout the state agree that Overstreet will be one of the most highly recruited athletes in the nation after this season. Down at Judge Bennett's Restaurant and Grocery, there is constant coffee cup speculation over where he will attend college. David himself remains very close-mouthed about his ultimate choice, saying only that he thinks he has the field narrowed to "five or six."

For the present, however, college still seems a long way off for the powerfully built teen-ager. His concentration is centered on the game against New Diana, just hours away.

Long before kickoff time, the stadium adjacent to Big Sandy High School is filled to capacity, vibrating with the kind of anticipation only small-town Texas schoolboy football generates. The entire population of the community, right down to the youngest infant, appears to have congregated to cheer their adolescent heroes. Judge Bennett is there. So is Kenneth Boles from down at the bank, and Johnny Johnson who runs the Exxon, and Rooster Reville who is retired. They quickly form a huddle and offer small wagers. Jim Bradley, who played for the Wildcats in the '40s and now works for a refinery in Fort Worth, has driven over for this game as he has so many others in the past. Butcher-paper banners, handmade by the cheerleaders, hang in front of the BSHS band section, urging the Wildcats to prove themselves again No. 1.

And indeed in this 1976 season the Wildcats have some proving to do. Last year's perfect season set a new state team scoring record of 820 points (an average of 58.6 points per game) and won Big Sandy the Class B championship, so the University Interscholastic League, governing body of Texas high school football, elevated the team to Class A when it was determined the high

112

school's enrollment would increase beyond the 126 student maximum allowed Class B participants. That enrollment boom had come about when nearby Ambassador College, one of the two Worldwide Church of God institutions directed by Garner Ted Armstrong, decided to discontinue its on-campus high school for the youngsters of faculty members. Although there are now 28 more boys in Big Sandy High (there are 81 in all, 47 of them out for football), Coach Norman and his Wildcats did not gain a single new recruit, since the newcomers hold to a faith which has the Sabbath begin at sundown on Friday and run through sundown Saturday. Thus it is a violation of their religious beliefs to participate in Friday night football games.

Suffice it to say they are not missed on this particular Friday. The Wildcats score on their first two possessions, Overstreet dashing 70 yards for a touchdown the second time he touches the ball. Before the night ends he will have rushed for 189 yards on 14 carries, returned a punt for a touchdown (called back because of a penalty), made a touchdown-saving interception from his defensive middle linebacker position, and led Big Sandy to a 26-0 victory—its 43rd game without a defeat.

Standing in the steamy dressing room, surrounded by his weary but happy squad, Jim Norman towels the sweat from his broad forehead and reflects back to a half-time speech he made, one in which he was unusually critical of the Wildcats' performance.

"Fellas," he says, "I chewed on you pretty good at the half. But I didn't think we were playing the kind of ball Big Sandy is capable of playing. I don't know, maybe I expect too much of you guys. Maybe I'm demanding too much. You'll have to let me know."

A mixed chorus of voices assures him such is not the case.

"You went out there in the second half and got the job done," he continues. "I'm proud of you. And remem-

113

ber this: I may get on you and I may criticize you—but if anyone else tries to do it he's got me to deal with. I love every one of you ... "

With that the lights are turned out in the locker room and a hush falls, broken only by a team member's high-pitched voice leading the squad in prayer.

As the players shower, Norman steps outside into the unseasonably crisp night with his three assistants. Most of the traffic has made its way out of the parking lot. The field lights have been turned off. A near-full moon hangs in the sky, casting elongated shadows on the turf where the Wildcats have just successfully opened their home season. For a few moments the coaches stand in collective silence.

Norman, his hands buried in his pockets, looks out toward the field. "Someday," he says, "we're not going to be so lucky. Someday we're going to lose. That's why we've got to play this game just for the fun of it. It's got to be fun or it's no good. Remember that."

And then he turns, another September Friday completed, and slowly walks back toward the field house.

ring. For 53 straight football Friday nights, the
n's lost. They lost 7-6 heartbreakers and were beaten
adly once (99-0, by Orangefield) that the coach opted
ave town the following morning. In this community
76, where Sunday-go-to-meetin' and Double Stamp
down at the Brookshire Brothers Grocery are con-
d major social events, only those on hand back on
nber 9, 1977 could boast of the special honor of
cheered for a Lions victory. On that long ago eve-
collection of players long since graduated de-
earby Woodville, 7-2.

ce Carnahan of the National Federation of State
chool Associations headquartered in Kansas
souri, is quick to point out that his organization
dwell on negative records but admits, "the
osing streak is the longest we're currently
There is an 8-man team in Kansas which had,
rt, lost 45 in a row. That's the closest anyone
Kountze."

call recently from a school up in Oregon,"
Moore, editor of the weekly *Kountze News*,
why we've kept on playing. They had lost 49
re deciding to just do away with their foot-
Obviously, they didn't understand the im-
ed on high school football here in Texas."
chool superintendent Robert Hunt, hired
years ago, had never seen the Lions win.
ayfield, owner of the local feed store, re-
that 1977 win, just weeks after moving
ity. He also remembers watching two
years without ever enjoying a victory.
members of the team recall attending
Lions won, back when they were just
gh.

frustrating," admits Ed Bumstead,
nt & Body Shop, booster club pres-
senior tackle, Joe. "When you've got
a senior and he's never had the expe-

118

8

*"There was a time when we tried to keep up
with negative records, like who had lost the most
games in a row. But, those who held them weren't
exactly thrilled about it so we stopped several years
ago. Now, we only keep positive records. And it's
probably best. No one wants to be remembered for
fumbling ten times in a single game or breaking the
national mark for most interceptions in a season..."*
— Bruce Carnahan,
National Federation of
State High School Associations

THE NIGHT THE VICTORY BELL RANG

In the fall of 1982, reminders of the almost forgotten
woes of win-starved Asherton High School came flooding back. In a world which celebrates its winners with
trophies, headlines, banquets and ticker-tape parades,
the loser, I once again realized, is still forced to scratch
for his own rewards.

Thomas Edison High School in North Philadelphia,
the morning paper told me, had endured five straight
seasons without a single victory. Since 1977 the Inven-
tors' only cause for celebration had been a 6-6 tie with
Simon Gratz in October of '78. Worse, they had suffered
through 27 straight games — 111 quarters — without the
satisfaction of a single point scored.

115

Then, however, Coach Roger Jann's forces came from a 12-0 deficit to score a 20-18 victory over University City High. "When we scored our first touchdown," Jann said, "it was like a dark cloud was suddenly lifted. When we finally won the game it was the greatest relief I've ever felt. Amazingly, the kids were very subdued in the dressing room afterwards. It was as if a giant weight had been lifted from their shoulders, knowing the losing streak was finally out of the way."

Down in Bullard, Texas, meanwhile, the coach and players were still looking ahead to that feeling. A basketball power for years, the school had decided to field a football team three years earlier. Some were still questioning the judgment of that decision when, as the '82 campaign came to a close, the team's record was 0-30. And the prospects for '83 were less than encouraging.

Neither Thomas Edison nor Bullard, however, knew the hard times of Kountze (Texas) High where a generation of students had traveled through the academic maze of high school and graduated, never having seen their team win a single football game.

When I phoned Hal Wingo, a transplanted Texan who still admits to a fondness for the caliber of football played in his home state, suggesting a trip to Kountze to do a story for his *People* magazine, he first hedged. "Everybody knows the best high school football in the world is played in Texas," he said, showing his true colors. "How's it going to look if we print a story about the worst team in history?"

"Hal," I said, "they just might win. This Friday is Homecoming. The time's right."

"It's a good story either way," he finally admitted. "Go ahead."

And so it was that I was off to pay a visit to another loser, hoping this time it would be my good fortune to be there on . . .

The Night The Victory Bell Rang

It was the manner of high drama a
school football fields throughout the S
autumn Friday night. With an enth
ing crowd looking on, the host tea
against its visiting rival but penalti
fortune had prevented their scorin

Thus, as the final seconds tic
clock, a rare 0-0 tie looked all bu
ties are greeted with only sligh
outright country licking.

With just seconds remaini
Kountze High School Lions
fumble — which enabled seni
a 27-yard field goal with o
give his team a 3-0 victory,
any this tiny lumber mill

For the Lions, it wa
the opening game of dis
was something that w
rival Kirbyville.

It was, instead,
infamous period in h
as the losingest hi

On the night
tration-filled yea
a winner . . .

Several y
dramatic sh
Kountze Bc
commodati
ished it, n
Its funct
after an

Th
dium
agair
field

rience of winning even one game, you get a little impatient with it all. But all you can do is just keep supporting them, keep hoping."

Support is something the community has freely given. Despite the dismal history, the stands at the high school stadium west of the town are generally filled. When the Lions traveled to an out-of-town game recently, no fewer than 600 Kountze residents followed.

The losing streak, longest in the storied history of Texas high school football (Beeville High previously held the record, losing 41 straight from 1970 to 1974), had begun to gain the school more nation-wide publicity than any positive accomplishments. Never mind that the girls volleyball team had won state championships in three of the last four years and claimed two recent district basketball titles. The Streak, as it had come to be called, was what Kountze was famous for.

And there were times when it seemed no amount of local support and optimism could ever bring it to an end. Three years ago the townspeople began a "We'll Be There When The Victory Comes" campaign, complete with T-shirts and bumper stickers. When, however, the bumper stickers were delivered to Bumstead the first thing he noticed was that the printer had mis-spelled Kountze. "That," he says, "was the way things had been going around here for a long time."

As the Lions were preparing to host Kirbyville the negative signs were again very much in evidence. First, it rained on the Homecoming Parade. Later that evening, just before kickoff, the wiring in the stadium's bank-sponsored scoreboard briefly went out. And the hand-painted paper banner the Kountze High cheerleaders had prepared ripped before the team had the opportunity to make the traditional run through it onto the field. Clearly, the fates held no sympathy or favor for Texas' losingest high school.

Add the fact that starting quarterback Tommy Joe Bumstead (no relation to booster club president Ed) had

119

suffered a broken collarbone in the previous week's loss and would not play, and chances for the long-awaited victory again seemed slim.

Still, optimism prevailed. Don Elliff, the 33-year-old coach of the Lions who is in his second season in Kountze, had all but assured those gathered at the Thursday night pep rally-bonfire that this was the week the streak would end. His wife, Connie, felt so good about the team's chances that she made plans to leave a note congratulating her husband on his first win in his car *before* the game, so he would find it when leaving the school parking lot later that night.

Elliff, the fifth head coach Kountze has had since the streak began, had taken the job last year after serving as an assistant at five other high schools. A halfback of modest ability during his own high school days and later as a non-scholarship participant at Southwest Texas State despite his 5-4, 130-pound frame, he had sought the Kountze job because of the challenge it offered.

"A friend of mine who was aware of the situation here told me it would be a great place to begin my head coaching career," he says. "He told me if I could come here and manage to win one, I'd be on my way. I looked into the situation and found that the attitude of the community was, under the circumstances, tremendous. What they were looking for was someone who would come in and stay around long enough to get the program re-established."

It has taken longer than he had hoped. As he prepared his team for the Kirbyville game, he had only a two-season string of 15 losses to his credit.

"I don't sense that anyone's gotten down on him," said Mayor Mayfield as he sat drinking coffee down at the Top Half Restaurant Friday afternoon with several other Kountze High supporters. "He's brought a lot of enthusiasm to the program and he's a hard worker. And, most important, he seems determined to see this thing through, to turn things around. I admire what he's done."

"This year's team," added Superintendent Hunt,

"has shown a lot more enthusiasm and ability. We've not been outclassed by anyone we've played this year. It's just a matter of time. Maybe even tonight."

James Read, a long time follower of the Lions, admitted that he has, since the season began, been carrying two large Roman candles he saved from his Christmas-July Fourth fireworks business in the trunk of his car and would, even at the risk of arrest, set them off whenever the Lions won.

"I'm proud of the way the townspeople have stood behind the kids and the coach," says school board president Roy Langston. "And the student participation has been great. You ought to go to one of the pep rallies. Shoot, there are towns around here that, if their team lost a couple of games, you wouldn't see 25 people in the stands the next Friday night. Our turnouts have always been good, rain, cold, whatever."

"That's the kind of attitude this community has," says Elliff, who is seated in a nearby booth with assistant coach Ted Daniel, going over his game plan one last time before returning to the field house for the pre-game team meeting. "Oh, there was a little negative criticism when I first arrived, but we've just about eliminated that. Once we get the streak behind us, things will be okay. We've been close on several occasions lately — but close counts only in horseshoes and hand grenades."

While Elliff has, since his arrival, maintained an outward show of enthusiasm, private moments have found him in a different frame of mind. "There have been times when he's really been discouraged," says Connie. "Sometimes after a game he and the other coaches will stay up at the school until two in the morning, trying to figure out what to do next, wondering why they ever got into the coaching business in the first place. But, then, in a couple of days he would be up again, ready to begin preparing for the next game."

Senior Troy Stratton, one of the 24 players on the 1982 Lions squad, has not seen the disenchanted side of his coach. "We'd like to win and get all this talk about the losing streak behind us," says the 17-year-old Student Council president. "We just inherited it, you know. Same as Coach Elliff. We haven't lost 53 straight games. We want to end it, though; for ourselves and for Coach Elliff."

And for other reasons. "There are a few kids in school—not many—who put the guys down for losing all the time," says cheerleader Kim Hart. "Sometimes they make it difficult at the pep rallies. It's been just as frustrating for the cheerleaders. But we keep trying to come up with ways to keep the spirit up. And Coach Elliff has helped us a lot. We all think he's great."

"I know this," says young Stratton, "he's the best coach I've had since I started playing. The guys on the team respect him, and he believes in us."

One of the primary lessons Elliff has tried to teach his team is to maintain its poise. On Friday night, in those final, hectic moments against Kirbyville, his lessons would pay off.

Long after senior Kathy King had been crowned Homecoming Queen and the band had played and the public address announcer had saluted a local couple in attendance who were celebrating their 49th wedding anniversary, the Lions were still in the battle, locked in a scoreless defensive struggle.

"None of those guys are going to be happy with a tie," said former Kountze All-State halfback Gordon Gilder, a member of the 1967 Lions team which advanced to the state semi-finals before it suffered defeat. "If you're gonna break a streak like that, you've got to do it with a win."

Gilder is another who is pleased with the progress Elliff has made. "He seems like a good coach and the kids seem to believe in him. That's a big thing. He's got things headed in the right direction. I've got the feeling the losing is about to end," the Kountze auto dealer says.

122

It would be a fumble recovery by junior tackle David Kelly with just 36 seconds remaining that would mark the beginning of the end of the streak. Thirty seconds later Wally Whisenhant came on to kick the field goal that would earn the Lions their victory.

No sooner had the ball cleared the uprights, most of the 1,300 on hand poured out of the stands and onto the field. James Read set off his Roman candles, and players who had been kneeling in prayer on the sidelines seconds before the field goal attempt, rushed onto the field to join the celebration. Coach Elliff, overcome by the emotion of the moment, fell to his knees and started crying. "My mind just went blank," he said. "We needed that win so badly. I just couldn't help myself. For a minute there, I was bawling like a kid."

In time the officials managed to clear the field so the final three seconds could be played out before the victory was official. That accomplished, the celebrating began anew.

Once in the dressing room, Elliff congratulated his players and rushed to his office to phone the happy news to the wire services who had requested a call whenever his team finally won. Hugging his four-year-old daughter Jessica, he told of the victory, calling it "the greatest moment of my coaching career." Minutes later he and his assistant coaches were being thrown into the shower by members of the team.

Standing to one side in the dressing room, holding the ball his son had kicked just minutes earlier, was Gene Whisenhant. "I've never been so proud in my life," he said. "I just had to come in here and pat my boy on the back. He and all the others have worked so hard for this. So have the coaches. And the people in the community."

Himself a graduate of Kountze High and a member of the team in the early '50s, Gene Whisenhant, like so many others, had seen the 53 defeats first-hand. "No way I was going to miss a game," he said, "and have 'em win when I wasn't there. This night is going to be something this town will remember for a long, long time."

Outside, the rains that had threatened all evening finally came. Yet people — parents, ex-students, students, girlfriends, coaches' wives — stood, waiting, still cheering.

"There's a dance in the school gym after every home game," Elliff said as he toweled off from his impromptu shower. "This one will be the first victory dance we've ever had."

With that he fell silent, listening. "Can you hear that?" he asked. "Doesn't that sound great?"

Over the cheers, from across the parking lot in the stadium, the Victory Bell was finally ringing.

The reaction to the story, which was squeezed into an issue which dealt considerably more attention to the relationship of Prince Andrew and his soft-core porn love, Johnny Carson's talent coordinator, and a new Broadway show which starred people dressed as cats, was interesting.

Proving once again that most in the world love a winner and sympathize with a loser, Kountze High and Coach Elliff were dealt high praise and congratulations. From most points.

The author of the piece, in fact, was the lone target of criticism. Despite a concerted effort to be certain Kountze was, in fact, the rightful owner of the longest losing streak on record, he overlooked the Lone Pine (Calif.) Eagles and was properly reminded by an irate letter which appeared in *People* the following week:

"For your information," the writer pointed out, skipping over the salutations, "the Kountze High School football team did not have 'the longest losing streak in recent history.' The Lone Pine Eagles had lost 54 games in a row when they scored a forfeit win over Death Valley High on September 24. This is a dubious honor, but Lone Pine did hold the record."

I saw no good reason to suggest that the Lone Pine record had come to an end well before that of the Kountze Lions, so opted neither to answer nor argue.

124

"He is obviously a great young athlete, one of the best our country has. But I will not remember Johnny Jones for the victories he won or the honors he attained. I shall remember him as one of the most generous people I've every known of."
— *Eunice Kennedy Shriver,*
president of the Special Olympics

WELCOME HOME JOHNNY JONES

It is something of a tradition in American sport that most athletic pursuits are comfortably retained within certain boundaries. A brilliant high school football player, for instance, is fully expected to perform well against his peers, his own age group. But put a sixteen-or seventeen-year-old kid in a college game and he would suddenly become what he is — a boy among young men. Taking it a step further, college athletes are judged a step below professionals. To be sure, there is sound logic to the boundaries of competition.

When, however, a youngster ignores those boundaries, performing at a level far beyond his years and experience, it is not only noteworthy but just cause to believe in magic.

Such was the case that summer of 1976 when Johnny Jones, a quiet youngster from the Central Texas town of Lampasas, defied all the rules of logic and gained a station reserved for only a select few. At age 18, recollec-

125

tions of high school football heroics, basketball victories and blue ribbon track performances still fresh on his mind, he achieved the impossible. He returned home from the Montreal Olympic Games with a gold medal. Competing against the best sprinters the world has to offer, he finished sixth in the 100-meter dash final, then ran a leg on the United States' victorious 400-meter relay.

Clearly, he was something special. What, I wondered, had powered him to such lofty heights at so young an age? And how would his friends and neighbors greet him on his return from the sports world's most glorified event?

In hopes of finding some answers and getting a first-hand look at a young man who had done something I personally regarded as one of the most amazing sports achievements in modern history, I made it a point to be on hand along with the citizens of Lampasas to say . . .

Welcome Home, Johnny Jones

Only 20 hours earlier, in a drizzling rain in Montreal, he had stepped proudly to the top level of the awards stand to have an Olympic gold medal placed around his neck. At age 18, Johnny Jones had accomplished what sports world Walter Mittys spend a lifetime dreaming of. The 70,000 on hand in the ultramodern Olympic Stadium erupted into a thundering cheer as Jones and his three American teammates were introduced as members of the winning 4 x 100-meter relay. Standing on their right was the second place East German team; on their left, Russia, winner of the third place bronze medal.

At that moment, with the national anthem playing, the American flag being raised, with the oversized gold medal hanging from his neck, a wide smile broke across Johnny Jones' face. The youngest Texas athlete ever to earn a berth on a U.S. Olympic track and field team, he was suddenly an international celebrity. A week earlier he had become the first American high schooler to reach the Olympic 100-meter finals since a Glendale (Calif.)

High senior named Frank Wykoff managed the feat in 1928. Running against the fastest sprinters in the world, Jones had finished in sixth place. Then had come the victory in the relay on the next-to-last day of the Games. Following the awards ceremony there was much celebrating, a great flood of relief, and little sleep.

Back home in Lampasas, Texas, where little ever happens to interrupt the slow-paced life-style, most of the 7,000 townspeople had zealously heeded the words on a downtown marquee — "Watch Johnny Jones Run in the Olympics" — urging them to see it all happen, to watch, through the magic of electronics, one of their own accomplish what so many had said was impossible. They sat glued to their television sets looking on as young Jones, the same soft-spoken kid who had been scoring touchdowns for the Lampasas High School Badgers just a few months earlier, became an Olympic champion. On that particular July Saturday afternoon downtown business had come to a standstill. The lone movie theater was doggedly playing a Walt Disney film to an almost deserted house. Few ripples were being made at the municipal pool. John Storms, a distant relative of the young Olympian, closed down his service station, and even the Dairy Queen, normally the site of buzzing teen-age activity, was graveyard quiet. Everyone was at home watching television, waiting impatiently for the finals of the 4 x 100 relay, anxious to see local history being made several thousand miles away. They watched, they cheered, they marveled at the accomplishment — and they waited to welcome him home.

Long before his trip to Montreal Johnny Jones had become something of a schoolboy legend in the Central Texas sporting community. In his final two years of high school he had scored 45 touchdwns and had been selected to the all-state football team. From numerous scholarship offers, he chose to sign an agreement to continue his athletic and academic pursuits at The University of Texas in Austin. Despite playing part of the last season with a broken finger, he had been a standout member of the LHS basketball team. Then, in the spring his fancy turned to track and even more amazing performances. He was the defending state Class AAA 440-yard dash champion, and had not run a competitive 100-yard dash since junior high days. Nonetheless, because of his outstanding showings in the quarter mile, Jones' coach, Scott Boyd, began to ponder what his young pupil might be able to do in the shorter sprint events.

Thus one day early last March Boyd informed Jones that part of his regular afternoon workout would be spent running a 100-yard dash for time. Johnny responded by covering the distance in 9.29 seconds — less than .3 of a second off the world record. Boyd, certain that his clock must be wrong or the 100-yard course laid out on the school's dirt track was too short, masked his amazement and suggested another time trial the following day. In the meantime he personally re-measured the track and summoned an assistant coach to also time the 100. This time Jones ran 9.24.

Suddenly Boyd, a reserve quarterback during his days at The University of Texas, realized he had a youngster who promised to be the greatest sprinter in Texas schoolboy history. Maybe even an Olympic candidate. He wasted no time in entering Jones in the sprints at weekend invitational meets.

Johnny, despite never having spent the long hours generally required to perfect the swift start so crucial to spring success, began running mind-boggling times. In his first competitive 100 at the Brownwood Bluebonnet Relays he recorded a 9.18. Later in the district meet in Round Rock he stunned the crowd with a 9.05, just .05 of a second off the world 100-yard dash record, and set a new state high school record in the 220 with a 20.7. Along the way he also managed to become the leading long jumper in the state with a leap of 24 feet, one-quarter inch.

It was at the Class AAA state meet in Austin, however, that Johnny Jones had his finest hour. After easily winning the 100 and 220, he prepared to run the anchor leg for the Lampasas High mile relay. A first place finish in the event would earn the Badgers the coveted state championship. Jones took the final handoff in seventh place, 40 yards behind the leaders. It appeared to be a hopeless situation. In the middle of the Memorial Stadium backstretch the smooth striding youngster began his move. The 15,000 spectators were mesmerized. The public address announcer began detailing Jones' every step: "He has moved up to fifth . . . he's fourth . . . third . . . " Into the final straightaway he still trailed the two leaders, but an amazing burst down the homestretch propelled him past the last two runners, and he hit the tape five yards in first place. The crowd went wild, pouring out of the stands to offer congratulations.

A reporter cornered a jubilant coach Boyd and asked him what the talented youngster could possibly ever do that would surpass the performances he had just completed. Boyd, holding the championship trophy in his arms, smiled. "He's going to take a shot at making the Olympic team."

The people of Lampasas, now convinced that Jones was capable of accomplishing whatever he set his mind to do, immediately set out to make sure he had the opportunity to qualify for the mid-summer U.S. Olympic Trials. To qualify, a runner must meet a specified time standard over the Olympic metric distances. Since Jones had been running only yards all spring he would have to compete in some meets where metric distances would be run. That meant travel to some of the nation's major meets where he would not only run the required distances but also would face far better competition than he had been running against during the high school season. It meant entering the Martin Luther King Freedom

Games in Atlanta, the Steve Prefontaine Classic in Eugene, Oregon, and the National Junior AAU in Knoxville, Tennessee. Such travels would have to be financed. Lampasas dentist Jack Baum and local federal land bank official Johnny Roberson solved that problem in a matter of days, heading a fund-raising committee which presented Boyd with a check for $3,500. The coach and his star sprinter thus were equipped to begin a summer-long quest for a spot on the Olympic team.

In his first venture into major league competition in Atlanta, Jones, running only the 400 and 200 meters, placed fifth and third, respectively. The organizers of the meet had blocked his competing in the 100, pointing out to Boyd that they had limited the field to "only topnotch performers." Meet officials in Eugene a week later were less hesitant to allow the still relatively unknown schoolboy to compete in the 100. Running on a rain-soaked track, he won in 10.44. Another week later in Knoxville he blazed to a 10.1 and thus became eligible to compete in the Olympic Trials.

But despite his impressive performances, college coaches, veteran Olympic observers and knowledgeable members of the sporting press still gave Jones little chance of being a part of the massive athletic carnival in Montreal. He was, they insisted, too young (he had turned 18 only in April), too inexperienced to handle the overwhelming pressure that goes with making a bid for a spot on the U.S. Olympic team. Then too, he was attempting to make it in one of the Games' glamor events, the one which would ultimately determine who would become internationally recognized as the World's Fastest Human.

Jones and his coach ignored the negatives and packed their suitcases for the Olympic Trials in Eugene in late June. There would be more than 40 other sprinters on hand, all hoping to survive the qualifying heats and reach the eight-man, 100-meter dash final.

"I think," remembers Boyd, "that the first time I became certain that Johnny was, in fact, going to be able to handle the pressure of competing against older, more experienced runners came right before the first preliminary heats of the 100. All the sprinters were gathered on the track behind the starting line, awaiting their lane assignments. All except Johnny. He was just sitting in the infield close by with his hands on his knees. Now remember, this was the best collection of sprinters in the United States and Johnny looked relaxed, totally unawed by the situation. At that moment I became even more firmly convinced that he had a good chance of making the team."

To those who witnessed the Lampasas youngster's advancement to the finals, he was virtually unknown. The sheer fact that he was able to survive the preliminary heats and reach the finals was a noteworthy accomplishment in itself—yet there were still few who felt Jones had a chance to be among those outfitted for a U.S. Olympic team uniform. The top three finishers in the final would form the American contingent in the 100 meters at Montreal. The fourth place finisher would be taken as an alternate for the sprint and would be the most likely candidate to round out the four-man 400-meter relay team. Eight runners went to their marks to dash for the coveted spots.

It was over in 10 seconds. National collegiate champion Harvey Glance, an Auburn freshman, broke from the blocks ahead of the pack and snapped the tape ahead of 19-year-old Florida standout Houston McTear, co-holder of the world 100-yard dash record. Twenty-four year old Steve Riddick of Philadelphia was an eyelash back in third. And in lane seven the surprising Jones, recovering from a poor start, lunged his 6-0, 175-pound body forward to finish in fourth place. It had taken him 10.23 seconds to gain the status of an Olympian.

In a matter of days his position on the team would become even more solid. In addition to being selected to run the second leg of the 4 x 100 meter relay, he would be elevated to the number three spot on the 100 meter entry list, since McTear, who had suffered a severe muscle pull at the finish line in the trials, was judged by the team doctors unable to compete in the Olympics.

Lampasas mayor James Hoffpauir sat in his office at the local Chevrolet dealership, studying the gold-painted wooden key to the city he had had prepared to present to Johnny Jones upon his return home. "We've never presented one of these before," he said, "so I'm not sure what it is supposed to look like."

Several local businessmen visiting in his office assured him that it looked fine, that it was, after all, the thought that counted. Certainly the leaders of Lampasas, Texas, had been giving considerable thought over the past weeks to how best to welcome their Olympian home. Plaques had been prepared, proclamations drafted, speeches written. Johnny's track shoes which he had worn in the state meet were being bronzed, and one would be presented to him, the other to his mother. Coach Boyd, back from Montreal after watching Johnny in the 100 meters, and before flying to Houston for a coaching school, also helped with the preparations. He said he would have the Lampasas High jersey Johnny wore in the Olympic Trials placed in the school trophy case. The high school band and drill team were alerted. All over town kids were painting "welcome home" signs. Bob Sutton, president of the First National Bank, volunteered the bank's private plane to fly to Dallas to meet Johnny's commercial flight from Montreal, which was due to arrive at mid-morning on Sunday.

Saturday Johnny had been awarded his gold medal. "That," said dentist Baum, grinning, "makes it perfect. Now we're not only honoring Lampasas' first Olympian; we're honoring our first gold medal winner." "Johnny Jones Day" would be perfect.

A sizable crowd was on hand at the tiny airstrip just north of town well before the private plane's scheduled 1:30 p.m. return from Dallas. Clearly, there were few in town who wanted to miss paying tribute to the youngster who had brought their city international recognition.

"I bet I've heard the word 'Lampasas' on TV 10 or 15 times in the past couple of weeks," an elderly black lady, shaded by a giant umbrella, said. "Can't buy publicity like that," her companion replied. "No way."

The idle conversation turned into an excited hum as a small plane appeared on the horizon. "That's him," an excited youngster carrying a homemade banner reading "Way to Go Johnny!" said. All eyes turned skyward, enthusiasm mounting as the plane taxied down the runway.

In the cramped quarters of the plane, Johnny, dressed in jeans and polo shirt, his USA team cap on his head, looked out the window of the plane and shook his head. His mother, who had flown home with him from Montreal, began to laugh. "Son," she said, "you had better start thinking of something to say. Looks like those people are expecting you to give a speech."

Johnny's eyes focused on the speaker's platform which had been erected, and he felt his mouth go dry much as it had back in Eugene when he was lining up for the finals in the 100-meter trials. "Here," said Boyd who had flown into Dallas to accompany him home, "put this on. There are a lot of people in town who want to see it." He took the gold medal from the case which Mrs. Jones, a deputy sheriff in Lawton, Oklahoma, had carried on her lap since the trip began at 5 a.m. at the Montreal airport, and draped it around Johnny's neck. The youngster's mother, a divorcee, looked at that medal and smiled. "It looks good on you, no doubt about that." (Mrs. Jones and Johnny moved from Lampasas to Lawton when he was in the eighth grade. A year later her mother became ill and Johnny suggested he could return to Lampasas and live with his grandparents for a year to help out in whatever way he could. His mother agreed, and then, when Johnny began to enjoy athletic success, said it would be okay for him to complete high school there.)

As Johnny emerged from the plane, grinning broadly, the cheers could likely have been heard throughout a good portion of Lampasas County.

The poise which had carried him to a spot on the victory stand in Montreal remained intact until he reached the top step of the airport speaker's platform. There waiting to greet him were his grandparents, the retired Rev. Arthur Anderson and his wife Mary, with whom Johnny had lived since he was a ninth grader. Simultaneously they embraced the youngster as tears appeared in the corners of his eyes and flowed freely down his cheeks. The homesickness was over.

He sat between his mother and grandparents, sipping on a soft drink, as the ceremonies began. There was 1968 Olympic 100-meter champion Jim Hines, offering his congratulations and assuring the crowd that "this young man you are here to honor today will be the world's fastest human four years from now when the 1980 Olympics are held in Moscow." There was University of Texas football coach Darrell Royal, assuring the concerned fans that playing football was not likely to impair Johnny's career as a track performer. "I've heard a lot of people voice concern over Johnny's getting hurt playing football," he said. "Well, let me say this: For him to get hurt, somebody's got to catch him first—and there are only five men in the world who can do that at this point, and none of them plays football." The remark drew cheers and laughter. So did the one-liner from emcee Wally Pryor who apologized for the delay in the ceremonies: "Johnny would have been here a little earlier, but he decided to fly instead of run."

The crowd, ignoring the blazing Texas sun, listened attentively as the parade of speakers heaped praise on the honored guest. Then it was finally time for Johnny Jones to speak. If he had been pursuing a spot on the Olympic forensic team last summer he would have better spent his time at his old job of pumping gas at John Storm's service station. Taking the microphone, he said, "I'd just like to thank everybody for all the support you've given me and our team through the years . . . " There was a long pause and then, "I guess that's about all I've got to say."

His grandfather closed the ceremony with a lengthy, moving prayer, and the crowd began to disperse. A car waited to take Johnny, his mother and his grandparents away for a few minutes of privacy before the youngster was to attend a press conference.

At the Anderson home a crowd of friends, neighbors and relatives milled around awaiting Johnny's arrival. Several hams were in the oven. Everyone had, it seemed, a favorite story to tell about Johnny when he was younger. "I just want to hug his neck and give him a big ol' kiss," an aunt who had arrived from Killeen said. "I'm so proud of that boy I could just bust."

His mother, having gotten there earlier, was busy showing his gold medal around.

Johnny arrived in the company of three of his friends who had waited for him outside while he went through the torturous demands of the press conference. An uncle carried his bags to his bedroom, another rushed off to get him a cold drink. Everyone was talking at once. A wide grin seemed permanently pressed on his face.

They would go on for the better part of an hour, the congratulations, the good-natured gibes about not coming home with two gold medals, the demands for his observations on life in the Olympic Village and about other stars on the U.S. team.

Finally, the tired youngster located his grandmother alone in the kitchen. "Be okay if I sneak out for a little while?" he asked. "They guys want me to go shoot a little pool."

Mrs. Anderson understood. She understood that he was tired of crowds, of attention. She understood that he was 18 and had been away from home for seven weeks and that he was anxious to see his friends, to relax. "You go on and have yourself a good time. We'll be here when you get back." With that she kissed him on the cheek. "It's good to have you home," she said.

An hour later he was in the game room of a former teammate's home, shooting pool with several of his buddies. "I'll tell you one thing, Johnny Jones," said friend Jerry Milligan who will be a member of the Texas A&M football team this fall. "You may be an Olympic champion in track but you ain't nothing in pool. Rack 'em up."

"Johnny Jones Day" had finally turned into the kind of day any 18-year-old could enjoy. The pressures, the demands and the excitement of the Olympic Games were behind him. It was now time to relax, to slip back into a slow summer life-style for a few weeks before leaving for Austin and life as a collegian.

At the day's end, coach Scott Boyd sat in his small office in the high school field house reflecting on all that had taken place in the previous few months. "For a coach, it is a once in a lifetime experience. It's something I'll never forget."

Lowering his feet from the desk and standing up, he looked out the window to the dirt track where it had all started that day in March when he had, out of curiosity, suggested Johnny Jones try his hand at sprinting. He did not speak for a while, then slowly he shook his head. "It's hard to believe," he finally said. "that right out there we raised an Olympic champion."

In the years that followed, Johnny Jones would enjoy a successful collegiate career at the University of Texas, earning All-America honors as a wide receiver and performing well on the Longhorns track squad. Eventually, he would give up track to sign a professional football contract with the New York Jets where, today, he continues to make headlines.

Still, it was a gesture he made while in college, one which received little attention from a sporting media mostly concerned with times, distances and touchdowns scored, that most often comes to mind.

Involved in the Austin Special Olympics program for handicapped children, Johnny expressed the desire to do something more than officiate at the youngsters' meets and help with their coaching. He wanted to make a contribution of a more material nature.

And so he appeared one day in the office of Special Olympics director Denis Poulos and gave him the gold medal he had won in Montreal. Jones suggested that perhaps it could be auctioned off and the money earned used to help fund the program.

"Watching those kids," he said, "makes you aware of just how lucky you are. By giving them the medal I can give a part of myself."

The medal, and the gesture, Poulos would say later, were too valuable a contribution to be placed on the auction block. Instead, Johnny's gold medal is displayed at Special Olympics events, serving as inspiration to young boys and girls not blessed with the abilities of Johnny Jones.

I can imagine no nicer legacy.

10

"The enthusiasm for football is tremendous in Mexico. Already there's a great deal of participation and a lot of people turning out to watch their games."
— *Dallas Cowboys assistant coach Gene Stallings, following a visit with high school football coaches in Mexico City*

FOOTBALL ACROSS THE BORDERS

In the fall of 1982 I authored a collection of reflections from former Dallas Cowboys players titled, "Journey to Triumph," hoping it would be greeted with some enthusiasm by Texas sport fans in particular and maybe a displaced Cowboys fan here and there in such foreign countries as California and Rhode Island. It was, in the vernacular of the publishing business, a "regional" book. Suffice it to say I had no visions of celestial royalty payments or five-figure paperback sales.

It was, however, to become a book which opened new territories. A dozen titles into a book-writing career in which the word "bestseller" has not once been mentioned, "Journey to Triumph" became the first book I'd written to be published in a language other than the Mother Tongue.

Shortly after its American debut, word came from Mexico City that a publisher there was willing to fork over a few devalued pesos for the Spanish rights to the book. Thus was born "Jornada al Triunfo." And, despite the shaky financial status of our neighbors to the South, the book did reasonably well.

And for a relatively good reason. Football, it seems, is gaining in popularity in Mexico by leaps and bounds. In Monterrey alone there were over 13,000 youngsters, ages 6 to 16, participating on 117 teams in 17 different leagues. The high schools which do not offer football as part of their sports programs are now in the minority. National Football League games are Sunday favorites of Mexico TV viewers and the *Dallas Cowboy Weekly*, a publication with a circulation of 100,000 in English, reaches 300,000 with its Spanish language edition.

Were I blessed with better foresight, I might have seen the phenomenon coming. Thinking back, it was point-blank evident on the night I gathered material for a story which was titled . . .

Football Across The Borders

Even to the casual observer it was more than just another high school football game. How many visiting coaches, for instance, are given keys to the city in mid-field ceremonies just before the kickoff?

Then, *two* national anthems were played and, by request of the visiting team, the referees were bilingual. In the printed program, one team listed its players' weights in pounds, the other used kilos. And over the public address system, an English-speaking announcer described each play then handed the microphone to another announcer for the Spanish translation.

All these things happened one night several weeks ago when Texas high school football went international. Little Fort Worth Christian Academy, a private high school affiliated with the Church of Christ, played host to Centro Universitario Mexico, one of the dozen private high schools operating in Mexico City.

The game between youngsters who live 2,500 miles apart and who speak different languages, has since gained significance beyond the 24-20 victory the Christian Aca-

139

demy Cardinals scored over the Centro Bucks. At least one other Texas high school has matched up with another team from Mexico, and schoolboy football in some quarters is assuming a definite international flavor.

The Cardinal-Bucks game drew 1,500 spectators, including some Mexico City supporters of the Centro team and a few local Mexican-Americans, to Cardinal Stadium in northeast Fort Worth. It had come about only after months of planning between the two coaches and lots of hard work by the visiting team, whose members earned money to pay for their trip.

The game was the brainchild of Fort Worth Christian coach Dub Manis, 35, and his former coach at Abilene Christian College, Dee Nutt. Nutt, while acting as coach of the Mexican Olympic basketball team recently, had heard that Centro Universitario wanted to play football against a Texas high school. So when he returned to the United States, Nutt suggested that Manis get in touch with Antonio Alvarez, the Mexican school's 29-year-old head coach.

Manis did so. Then he met with Alvarez in Mexico City early last summer for a planning session, which was followed by a stream of correspondence. In late July, officials from the two schools got together during a coaching clinic in Lubbock and worked out dates for a home-and-home exchange. Alvarez would bring his Bucks to Fort Worth early in the season and Manis agreed to take the Cardinals to Mexico City during the Thanksgiving holidays for a November 24 re-match.

Word of the international contest spread through the Texas Independent Schools Conference, to which Fort Worth Christian belongs, and other league members became interested in arranging similar games. With the help of Manis and Alvarez, Trinity Christian Academy of Dallas was able to schedule a game against Mexico City's Preparatory School No. 3, using the high school stadium at Ferris, Texas. There is every indication that the milestone game in Fort Worth opened an

140

avenue that may become well traveled in the next few years.

To finance their trip to the United States, the 56 members of the Bucks' traveling squad spent the summer working at a variety of jobs so each could earn enough to buy his own $120 plane ticket (a special round trip fare arranged for the team). But for the re-match, the Fort Worth team was planning to travel to Mexico City by bus, Manis said, so the kids will have an opportunity to see the countryside.

"I'm a geography teacher," Manis added, "and I think this will be a real field trip for the team."

The association of the two athletic teams, in fact, has produced several other advantages aside from the sports contest. During their three-day stay in Fort Worth the Mexican youngsters sampled the life style of some of this country's teen-agers. The visitors were housed in the homes of Christian Academy players, toured a Fort Worth museum and planetarium, visited Six Flags Over Texas and saw a Texas Christian University football game. There was also a shopping spree in downtown Fort Worth for gifts to take back to friends at the 2,000-student school in Mexico City.

For Bucks coach Alvarez, the trip afforded a chance to learn, first-hand, more about the strategy and style of American football. A standout soccer player in his schoolboy days, Alvarez later was persuaded by a friend to try out for football at the University of Mexico. He made the team and for three seasons was the starting quarterback. A knee injury sidelined him in his senior year. That was when he began coaching the Bucks.

Unlike U.S. coaches, Alvarez is not a schoolteacher. He works as an accountant with a Mexico City air conditioning firm, and his coaching duties begin after his regular office workday. He has three coaching assistants — one an accountant, another who works in a clothing store and the third, a University of Mexico student. All four

141

coaches receive a small salary from the high school.

American-style football, Alvarez explained through an interpreter, was played in Mexico as early as 1929, but the game did not gain much popularity until about 1965. Today enthusiasm for football has grown so that the Bucks draw crowds of 3,000 to 4,000 spectators a week during the season. And in Mexico City a tabloid newspaper called *Deporte Grafico,* which carries stories only about football (from the schoolboy level to the professional Dallas Cowboys), is thriving.

Alvarez says telecasts of the Dallas Cowboys games have spurred his country's interest in football. "The people of Mexico adopted the Cowboys as their team," he said. "You should have seen the celebration in Mexico City when they won the Super Bowl in '77."

Alvarez related that he and other coaches have developed their teams by studying films of U.S. games, by attending coaching clinics in this country and visiting practice sessions and games that American teams play in the high school, college and professional leagues. Thus, the tempo of the game between Fort Worth Christian and Centro Universitario was no different from the matches played in other high school stadiums on fall weekends throughout Texas. It had been preceded by an ear-bursting pep rally in the Christian Academy gymnasium, a rally that was punctuated by Spanish football yells coming from the visiting team which sat in as guests.

After this warm up, the Cardinal cheerleaders led a continuous parade of yells during the game to "show the boys we're behind them." And on the other side of the field, an impromptu cheering section backed the Bucks. It was led by Juan Guerro, Mexico's consul in Fort Worth, and Enrique Sroka, a Mexico City businessman whose son plays on the Bucks team.

Time after time, from the small gathering of Mexicans came the chant in two languages, "Go, Go, May-he-co! Go, Go, May-he-co!"

After the game, coaches Manis and Alvarez watched the boys of the two teams gathered in the Christian Academy dining room. They were laughing and joking as they ate dinner and got ready to take in an all-night bowling party.

"You know," Manis said, "it's pretty hard to tell the winners from the losers."

That it was.

11

"We had a football program that beat almost anything you might find outside of Texas. We had 800 kids playing football in 18 elementary schools scattered around town. And eventually they all came to Abilene High. The reason our kids were good was because they wanted to be good.
— former Abilene High coach Chuck Moser

WHERE HAVE
ALL THE HEROES GONE

The truth of the matter is I'm nostalgic to a thundering fault. Willie Nelson aside, I'll take the music of the Fifties, thanks; am still a bit miffed that someone in Detroit saw fit to eliminate running boards from modern automobile designs; and find more and more that I hold the movies being aired on the Late, Late show in higher regard than those advertised on the marquee down at the Multiplex Cinema.

What it boils down to, I suppose, is that I grew up in a simpler, more innocent time than my own teen-age children and feel not at all cheated by the fact. You can have Dustin Hoffman-as-Tootsie, violence as art, and X-rated sizzlers. Give me James Dean and Natalie Wood and "Shane" and science fiction without all that blood-and-gore realism. I wouldn't trade Buddy Holly or even one member of the Platters for all the punk-junk acid rip-off rock you can collect into Central Park on Bargain Night.

So yes, I've arrived at the age where it is now expected, if not fashionable, to bore family and friends with occasional recollections of "the good old days." And here, I suppose, is as good a place as any to admit that in more than one late night comparison of bygone athletic achievement my speed has improved a step or two and minor triumphs have grown to semi-major proportions. It's part of the aging process; one of man's inalienable rights.

But, I stop short of class reunions. With no great effort I've cleverly side-stepped ten-year and twenty-year gatherings and have a plan already designed to keep me away from the thirty-year celebration. I simply do not wish to see old flames who did me wrong lo, those many years ago, have no interest in comparing waist and/or hairlines with a bunch of guys who have probably gone on to make a bundle in oil, gas, futures and the video game rage. For the most part, I prefer to remember my graduating class the way it was when it was still sweating out receipt of a diploma, before business world success and failures had been achieved.

Recently, though, a writing assignment made it necessary to return to those days, to seek out old friends who had, for some years, been little more than a signature on a Christmas card.

One of my first encounters was with an old buddy whose name I shall not, for good reason, make mention of here. "Hey, Carlton," he said as he grabbed my hand and began pumping for a gusher, "its' really good to see you. You doin' anything these days or are you *still* just writing?"

You see why I avoid reunions.

Still, there was a warm sort of pleasure that accompanied my search for those who, long ago, were a part of something special, the members of . . .

Texas' Greatest Team

The yellow school bus rolled into the oncoming darkness, headed toward Abilene, carrying with it a cargo of teen-age boys who just hours earlier had been celebrating the rewards of an undefeated Junior Varsity football season. Their prize had been a trip to Dallas and the historic old Cotton Bowl, there to witness the 1957 Class AAAA semifinals.

Now, however, a despondent quiet had settled in with the swaying rhythm of the joyless ride. Except for occasional brief, quiet conversation it was a return made in somber silence.

For most of us — sophomore members of the Abilene High School Junior Varsity — a dream of future glories had died just hours earlier. The chance to one day have our names associated with an achievement unmatched in schoolboy history had been stolen by Highland Park and a swift, lethal halfback named Jack Collins.

They had, with a 20-20 tie and one more penetration than the Abilene Eagles, been victorious, remaining alive to play another day (and eventually defeat Port Arthur for the '57 state championship). Abilene, on the other hand, was finished for the year. So, too, was a national record-setting string of 49 consecutive victories.

It had begun in October of 1954 and had lasted through three straight state titles until that December of 1957 when it appeared the Eagles were on their way to title number four. *Time* magazine had deemed it an accomplishment worthy of reporting. *Sports Illustrated* did a story on Abilene High, calling it an athletic dynasty. That was all pretty heady stuff for 16 and 17-year-old boys growing up in a medium-sized West Texas town. The Abilene High School Eagles, coached by Charles (Chuck) Moser, were, in the mid '50s, the team all others in the state of Texas were measured against.

As sophomore jayvee players, we had gone through our own season playing before token attendance on Saturdays with one-column mention in the Sunday papers. Then as our schedule ended and the varsity advanced

146

into the playoffs we inherited the glamorless drudgery of performing as the scout team, running the next week's opponent's plays against our celebrated elders. It was the price to be paid.

The next year, we were assured, the cheers would be ours. Seniors would depart, making room on the varsity for us to play our respective parts, however large or small, in the continuation of the never-before-accomplished string of victories.

Time and *Sports Illustrated* would be writing about us. Thirty thousand would come out to see us play for another state championship. It was a dream few who ever reported for high school football even dared; a dream that died that crisp afternoon in the Cotton Bowl. We collectively cursed Jack Collins and privately ached for our lost opportunity.

At the time, it didn't seem fair. A loss by penetrations hardly seemed a proper way to put such a victory string to rest. It was a helluva way to lose.

Through good fortune I have never been party to any real community disaster. No floods have ever run through my streets, no high winds have ever left me or my friends homeless. Yet I shall never forget the solemn mourning that befell the city of Abilene, Texas, that December of 1957.

But the passage of time is, indeed, a soothing balm. Now, 25 years after that cold and quiet bus ride, it is not the loss that is best remembered by longtime residents of Abilene. It is, instead, the glory of victories. As it well should be.

Bobby Jack Oliver, now owner of an electronics equipment firm near Dallas, was not a part of the Abilene High winning streak. The standout tackle who would win all-state honors as a schoolboy, then star at Baylor and go on to spend seven years laboring in the Canadian pro ranks, graduated the year before the string began.

He was, on the other hand, a part of it in a manner of

speaking. Great triumphs are not achieved without a foundation first being laid. Oliver was part of that foundation.

"At the end of my junior year," he recalls, "our coach, Pete Shotwell, retired. I remember the superintendent calling (halfback) Jim Millerman and me into his office one day to tell us the names of some of the coaches that were being considered for the job. He asked us what kind of a man we thought the members of the team would like best to have.

"I don't remember the names of any of the other coaches they were thinking about — and to be honest, neither of us, Jim nor I, had ever heard of Chuck Moser, but the superintendent said he was a winner. We told him he would be fine with us. What we wanted was a winner."

What they got was a slightly built native of Missouri, a man who walked with his shoulders ever hunched forward. His physical appearance was far from the stereotype the general public maintains of a high school football coach.

"We were impressed, though," says Oliver. "He wasn't as big as a minute but had, in his college days, been an all-conference linebacker. If a man that small could play linebacker on a major college level, we figured he had to be something special."

It goes without saying that Chuck Moser did indeed prove to be something special. In 1953, his first year as head coach of the Eagles, he lost two, a 7-6 decision to Pampa and to eventual state finalist Odessa. The foundation was set.

"We didn't really have a great deal more talent than we had had in previous seasons," Oliver remembers, "but he convinced us that we were better than most people. I never knew a man with such energy. He never missed a bet. He was always thinking about the future. For instance, after he took the job he set up regular Saturday morning meetings with the junior high coaches to teach them the system he wanted to use. What it finally amounted to was the fact that when you were in the

148

seventh grade you were learning the plays and philosophy you would eventually be exposed to when you got in high school.

"We lived near his house when he first moved to Abilene and he would call me every Wednesday night and invite me over to watch the replay of Notre Dame games on television. He would point things out to me, showing me mistakes the players were making. He coached every waking minute in some way or another."

He also possessed the ability to make youngsters want to play football. Bobby Jack Oliver, his first all-stater, is proof positive. "I had played junior high football and hated every minute of it," Oliver admits. "One of the high school assistants finally talked me into coming out in high school. I don't think, though, I was ever really sold on the game until Coach Moser came to Abilene."

His initial season behind him, Moser seldom had need for the Saturday escape he designed for post-game defeats. "When we would lose one on Friday night," says the man who now labors as an assistant at Texas A&M, "I'd make sure I didn't go to town the next day. I'd stay home and work in the yard."

For the next three years Moser had the best football record and the worst-looking yard in Taylor County.

The victory string would begin in his second year. There would be a feast of records (the 1956 team, for instance, scored 496 points in 14 games), post-season honors or players, and a steady stream of plaudits for Moser's abilities. At one point he could count over 30 of his players who were on athletic scholarships at various colleges. Players like Glynn Gregory, Jimmy Carpenter, Stuart Peake, Boyd and Rufus King, Jim Welch and David Parks would become familiar to any and all who paid close attention to Texas schoolboy football in those days.

"I've never been one to spend a great deal of time looking back," says Moser today, "but it's hard not to think about those days every now and then. Actually, it's impossible because I'm always running into kids I

149

coached. Just the other day, for instance, I ran into John Young. He was a great little guard and linebacker for me — weighing all of 170 pounds. He's now on the Houston Oilers coaching staff and doing an outstanding job with their specialty teams.

"I always get a good feeling when I see some of my old players. I'm amazed at how well they've done. They call or drop me a line. I've always said that one of the greatest rewards of coaching is to watch kids grow into men."

He points to Jim Welch, a youngster who scored two touchdowns in the 1955 state championship victory over a Charlie Milstead-led Tyler High team.

"Jim wasn't 175 pounds soaking wet in high school. He didn't even start for us until his senior year, but then, he went off to SMU, did a good job, gained some weight, and went on to play eight years (1960-67) for the Baltimore Colts. Oh, he had ability, but not that much more than a lot of kids. What Jimmy had in addition to talent was a tremendous desire to be as good a football player as he possibly could."

Aside from Oliver, who played high school ball at 220, Moser coached few players in his career (141 wins, 29 losses) who weighed 200 pounds. His quarterbacks in particular in the glory years were smaller than most playing the position on the high school level. Yet they got the job done.

It was little H. P. Hawkins' pass to all-state end Twyman Ash in the final minute of play which gained Abilene a 14-7 victory over Houston Austin in the 1954 state championship game.

Harold (Hayseed) Stephens would direct the Eagles to another state title and go across town to Hardin-Simmons where, under the coaching of Sammy Baugh, he would establish a number of NCAA passing records.

"We had some outstanding athletes back then," says Glynn Gregory, a former schoolboy All-America, SMU running back and ninth-round draft pick of the

150

Dallas Cowboys in 1960. "But I really don't think that was the reason we won so consistently. Coach Moser was the smartest coach I ever played under. He was one of those men far ahead of his time. I feel honored to have played for him.

"One of the things that always impresssed me about him was the fairness he showed everyone on the team. Like any team, we had some players with more ability than others, but that didn't matter to coach Moser. He encouraged everyone, starter or sub alike, and made everyone aware that we had a contribution to make to the team."

The only people who got a short stick during Moser's coaching reign were his opponents. "We were," says Oklahoma oilman Jimmy Carpenter, a former all-state halfback who rushed for 227 yards, scoring on runs of 94 and 62 yards in Abilene's 15-0 win over Corpus Christi Ray in the 1956 AAAA finals, "fortunate to be a part of his program. I honestly think Abilene High was pretty well ahead of its time back then. I'm talking about coaching techniques, equipment, facilities, the works."

To a degree Moser agrees. "Maybe we were a little more sophisticated in our approach." he admits. "Today it is much harder for one school to have much of an advantage over another. Everyone has top equipment, top coaching staffs, nice stadiums to play in. I think there has been a leveling off in that respect — and that makes it even harder for anyone to win over a long period of time like we did.

"And, of course, winning creates a lot of that so-called sophistication. In the time we were winning all those games in a row we had a lot of things going for us. During the time I was in Abilene the population doubled. The enrollment at Abilene High grew from 1,700 to 2,300. And football players didn't move away the way they do now. If you were a football player, you just didn't move out of Abilene in the '50s.

That changed, however, as the society seemed to become more mobile. I remember in the '60s we went down to play Midland Lee one season and four of their starters were kids we had had in our junior high program. It's harder to build a program if you're constantly losing the younger kids."

To have moved a prospective Abilene Eagle away in the '50s would have been judged a high crime. There were, in fact, almost constant rumors of importation of players.

A yellowed *Sports Illustrated* clipping, quoting Moser, sets that issue right: "We don't import players or move families," he told writer Don Parker. "But we do have a football program that beats almost anything you might find outside of Texas. We have over 800 kids playing football in 18 elementary schools scattered around town. They all come to Abilene High.

"You win a lot and people get the idea that the kids on your team are supermen or over-age ringers. Look, the team's average age is 16.9 years, the average weight is 180. The reason these kids are good is that they want to be good. They work at it and they work hard."

Even today Moser is hard pressed to select moments he treasures over others. "We had so many good things happen to us back then," he says, "that it's hard to pick out things like that.

"But, I guess there are things that stand out in my memory above some of the others. Like my first win at Abilene High. We had scrimmaged against Stamford (a Class AA school coached by Gordon Wood) and hadn't looked good at all. But we came back in the opener and beat a good Highland Park team. Then, of course, the loss to them four years later still comes to mind every now and then.

"I imagine one of the best games we ever played was in the '55 state finals when we beat a good Tyler team (33-13). Gregory was outstanding that day (rushing for 171 yards and two touchdowns). So was Welch. And our defense played very well. We had something like 350 yards rushing and they didn't get but about 50."

The single game which Moser admits pride in, however, did not win him a state title. Rather, it was the game in '57 which won him a ticket to the eventual defeat by Highland Park.

Amarillo High, coached by the late Joe Kerbel, had gone through the season unbeaten and ranked No. 1 in AAAA and was an overwhelming favorite to defeat Abilene High, a team with far fewer superstars than in years past, in the quarterfinals. Adding to the Sandies' advantage was the fact the game would be played in Amarillo.

"We had only one starter back from the '56 state championship team, and at the end of the year not a single one of our kids got a Southwest Conference scholarship offer," Moser prefaces. "Amarillo on the other hand, had something like 18 kids get college scholarships. I've always said the '57 Amarillo team was one of the best ever."

Having averaged almost 40 points a game with a devastating belly-option offense, the Sandies were stopped cold by the Eagles as a stunned crowd of 22,000 watched the visitors win, 33-14, to stretch their winning streak to 49 in a row.

"That had to be one of our biggest wins," Moser admits. "On paper there was no way we should have defeated Amarillo."

There are those who will tell you that the game was Moser's coaching masterpiece.

The following week, however, Highland Park won its penetrations victory to deny Moser and his Eagles a shot at a record fourth straight state title.

"It was a lot of fun back then," Moser says. "And, like the players, I'm proud of the things we accomplished. But not as proud as I am of what so many of those kids have grown up to be. They're good, solid citizens. Something rubbed off back there and that fact gives me a warm feeling."

Oliver, Welch, Gregory and end David Parks all enjoyed success as professional football players before settling into careers outside of athletics. Fullback Chuck Harrison went on to play major league baseball with the Houston Astros and several other clubs for a while.

Moser has kept close tabs. Twyman Ash is managing a restaurant in Port Arthur these days. Boyd King is the vice president of a steel manufacturing firm in San Antonio. His brother, Rufus, is in the insurance business in Houston. Stuart Peake is a Dallas doctor and Sam Caudle is doing quite well in Dallas as an investor. David Bourland owns and operates several service stations in Abilene, and David Parks now has opened a couple of health spas in Dallas. The list goes on.

"That makes it worthwhile," Moser says. "I was proud of those guys when they were kids playing high school football and I'm still able to say I'm proud of them as career men."

And the top classification of Texas high school football may never see again the kind of winning streak they put together back when the Abilene High Eagles and Chuck Moser were king.

12

"By definition, those kids are handicapped. But if you let yourself think about it, slack off for a second, your tail is whipped sure as shootin'. They make it pretty clear they have something to prove."

— a rival coach after a game
with the Texas School for the Deaf

THEY NEVER HEAR THE CHEERS

There will, I suppose, be a few purists who, having purchased this book for the sole purpose of reading about high school football, will wonder at the inclusion of the following piece. And it is, I guess, like slipping one orange into a sack of apples.

But since mixing apples and oranges has been a habit of mine for longer than most of the subjects written about in this book have been around, I shall continue. And will stubbornly offer no apologies.

It has been my observation that high school athletes, regardless of the sport they have chosen, attack their pursuit with a rare dedication. It was that fact which had drawn me to Austin one late fall afternoon, there to pay a visit to the Texas School for the Deaf. There was, frankly, more than a little curiosity about just how young athletes, healthy of body except for the eternal silence in which they live, approach their games.

And, yes, the original purpose of my mission was to do a story on the football program, seeking out answers

155

to the stock questions: How do the youngsters determine the snap count? Do they use sign language in the huddle, etc.?

But as I entered the school gym, hoping to locate someone who might steer me in the direction of the football coach's office, I was distracted at the trophy case. My plan changed as I reviewed the tangible mementoes of glories past.

Here, it seemed, basketball success had climbed to the national level. While the football team had enjoyed its moments of triumph against private school rivals, the TSD basketball teams had reigned as national champions on more than one occasion.

How, I wondered, was such a tradition built? How were the young men who played for the Texas School for the Deaf Rangers able to reach such levels when . . .

They Never Hear The Cheers

Just inside the red brick gymnasium in Austin, amid the smells of liniment and sweat, and the rhythmic thumps of a dribbled basketball, hangs a plaque honoring the young men who became High School All-Americans. There are 11 of them, dating back to 1934 when a 6-foot-1 forward named Buster Quinn was cited for his exceptional talents with a two-handed set shot.

Near the plaque hang photographs of the 1967-68 and the 1968-69 basketball teams — smiling, proud young athletes whose combined talents won them No. 1 rank among the country's schools for the deaf. The honors — the All-America citations and the prestigious No. 1 rankings — were bestowed by *The Deaf American* magazine, a California-based publication that is widely read on the campus of the Texas School for the Deaf (TSD) in Austin.

Here, in the evenings after supper and studies are completed, coach Prentis Ming gathers the 15 members of the current TSD Rangers team for rigorous practice workouts. Though they do not belong to any interscholastic league or conference, the Rangers play 18 regular

156

season games against three parochial and seven small public high schools in the Austin area and participate in three invitational tournaments.

Ming and his Rangers have the enthusiastic backing of the 650-member TSD student body. The 500-seat gymnasium on the campus is generally packed for home games, and the young fans are charged with the same kind of tensions and emotions you find at game time in almost every high school basketball gym. Five girl cheerleaders, snappily dressed in the school colors of white and blue, lead the student body in continuous sign language cheers, and lusty yells.

"People who aren't familiar with our program think our kids live in total silence," says athletic director Bill Snowden. "That isn't the case at all. Though only a few are able to speak (youngsters who learned to talk before they became deaf), they can yell — and, believe me. they do. They'll go through a cheer in sign language, then burst into yells.

"The players on the court can't actually hear them but they feel the vibrations generated by the noise, and it has the same effect. They are aware that their actions please their supporters."

The players' sensitive reactions to sound vibrations also have proved that the pre-game apprehensions of many men refereeing for the first time at TSD games were unfounded. "Our players know when the whistle blows," says Ming. "They can feel the vibrations or, on rare occasions when they don't, they see opposing players slowing down and realize at once that an official has halted the action for some reason.

During time-outs Ming does not launch into a booming tirade like many fellows in his profession. Instead, his fingers literally dance with the sign language he uses to point out flaws in the team's play and suggest improved tactics. To instruct a player during a game Ming uses a signal that alerts the entire team to look toward the bench. "If the particular player I want doesn't see me, another boy will let him know so he can look my way," says Ming. "It's no problem."

There was a time when the school, established by the Texas Legislature in 1856 for deaf students between the ages of 5½ and 21, had a hard time scheduling basketball opponents. Some schools were apprehensive about playing against a team of deaf athletes, and there also was concern because the TSD allowed 20- and 21-year-old students to compete on the high school level.

Before World War II, TSD had to schedule games with superior players. But the TSD has since adopted the Texas University Interscholastic League's (UIL) eligibility rules, which require players to maintain high academic standards and be under age 19 on September 1 when the school year begins.

Robert Hoover, TSD director of student life, explained that TSD students are generally older than those in comparable grades of public schools because the deaf students must undergo three years of special preparatory schooling before they can begin regular academic courses. "Our freshmen and sophomores, for instance, are often on the same age level as seniors in a public high school," he pointed out, adding that because of the 19-year-old eligibility rule many junior and senior students are too old for competitive high school athletics.

Although TSD is fully accredited academically by the Texas Education Agency and follows the UIL regulations for schoolboy athletics, the Rangers have not been admitted to UIL competition because of a rule which forbids participation by schools for the handicapped. But there is hope that the school might soon be admitted to the UIL. Says TSD athletic director Snowden, "I understand that serious consideration is being given to admitting private schools into the league at that time, and we hope to qualify on that basis. The deaf schools in states like Oklahoma and Mississippi already are participating in state leagues along with the public schools and they have no problems whatsoever."

Since the Rangers and coach Ming are barred at present from UIL play, their current goal is to build a record that will win them more honors among the nation's deaf schools.

Thirty-five-year-old Ming, who isn't deaf, is in his 13th year of coaching deaf youngsters. He came to TSD six years ago after a seven-year stint as assistant football and basketball coach at the Mississippi School for the Deaf. He became the TSD head basketball coach three years ago, and the assistant coaching job that Ming had held for three years at TSD went to Ray Piper, who is deaf and was once an outstanding athlete at the Oklahoma School for the Deaf.

Ming, an engaging person brimming with enthusiasm, teaches five classes of physical education and has been known more than once to challenge one of his players to a game of "one-on-one" (a basketball game employing one defensive and one offensive player) to establish the fact that he knows the ins and outs of the game. Ming played basketball at Arlington High in Philadelphia before earning a physical education degree at Southwest Texas State University in San Marcos.

"I took the job coaching at a deaf school because it paid $10 a month more than I was offered at a public school," he says. "I began, then, on a very selfish note, but I soon got wrapped up in it. The kids themselves taught me the sign language. And now I don't think there is any way I could leave to coach somewhere else. It would be like leaving home. I have a strong feeling about what I'm doing. It's a very satisfying job."

The TSD football, track and basketball teams have encountered no problems on the road. "People are always hospitable to us when we travel to compete with other schools," says Ming. "And they are, I think, a little surprised at the ability of our kids. They realize before the game is over that our boys are not nearly as handicapped as they might have thought."

The TSD athletic program strives for the same goals and results that schoolboy athletics promotes everywhere.

"Sports are good for kids," says Ming. "It's that simple. Any coach will tell you there are things you learn from athletics other than how to shoot free throws or kick a field goal. By learning the importance of competition, by giving maximum effort, by learning how to win and lose, a boy takes a step toward becoming a man.

"We work the players hard (basketball workouts last from 6:30 to 9 p.m.) and demand a great deal from them. Our rules are strict. It's a trite saying, but we feel that one is handicapped only when he lets himself believe he is handicapped. A deaf person can do anything physically that a hearing person can."

Hoover, the director of student life, also sees the athletic programs a great benefit to the school. He says, "A deaf youngster needs a way to prove he can compete with hearing kids. His confidence and pride get a boost when he realizes he can play against hearing kids and do a good job.

"The athletic program is important to the entire student body. It's not just the athletes who are involved."

Yet, seldom is a deaf athlete recruited for college sports teams. Sammy Oates, a standout basketball and football player at TSD in the mid '50s was an exception, attending Hardin-Simmons University in Abilene on a football scholarship. Though he could neither hear nor speak, his college athletic performances twice won him places on All-Border Conference teams and he was drafted by the then American Football League Houston Oilers. Today he is an executive with the Internal Revenue Service in Austin.

Gene Duve, who played on TSD's 1967-68 national championship basketball team, is now scoring points for

160

Gallaudet College, a Washington, D.C. liberal arts college for the deaf. He is working toward a degree and a coaching position in one of the nation's schools for the deaf.

Many TSD high school graduates enter vocational studies for the deaf at Lee Junior College in Baytown, Delgado Junior College in New Orleans or the National Technical Institute for the Deaf in Rochester, N.Y. And a number of the basketball players continue the game with the Dallas Silents or similar deaf club teams in Beaumont and Houston.

Ming was optimistic about the current team. "I think we are in a class to play with any school of comparable size anywhere," he said. "There's plenty of room to hang another team picture out there in the lobby."

ABOUT THE AUTHOR

Carlton Stowers, who was not nearly as good a high school athlete as he would like for you to believe, has authored over a dozen non-fiction books on subjects ranging from sports to the life story of Western movie hero Roy Rogers and his wife, Dale Evans. A prolific writer, he has authored pieces for a lengthy list of major magazines, serves as associate editor of the *Dallas Cowboys Weekly*, and produces a weekly pre-Olympic television show, "Countdown to '84," which is seen internationally.

He regrets that space in this book did not permit him to tell of his 96-yard touchdown run in the fading moments that lifted his team to a come-from-behind victory. Or how, had it not been for a less than perfect start, he just might have won the state 100-yard dash in his senior year.